CONTENTS

ACKNOWLEDGEMENTS

In preparing this edition my greatest debts are to Cecil Price's standard edition of Sheridan's works, and to F. W. Bateson, the first New Mermaid editor. I have also consulted with profit Michael Cordner's more recent edition. My debts to other scholars and critics I have attempted to acknowledge in the footnotes and Further Reading. I am grateful to the Bodleian Library, the University of Oxford, for permission to use as copy text the Tickell manuscript (MS. Don. d.174) and to reproduce its title page, and to the Houghton Library, Harvard University, for allowing me to quote from the Powell, 1779, and Scott promptbooks held in the Theatre Collection. The librarians at both universities were unfailingly helpful with my long distance enquiries and on my visits, and I am grateful to them and also to the staff at the Shakespeare Centre Library, and the National Theatre Archive. It is a pleasure to thank two former La Trobe colleagues, David Rawlinson and John Wiltshire, for providing answers to questions and for many discussions of the play, and also my copy editor, Sue Gibbons, for making numerous helpful suggestions, and Jessica Hodge at A & C Black for her prompt assistance. Brian Gibbons has been an exemplary General Editor, vigilant, and always encouraging. I owe much to his guidance; any remaining errors are my own.

Melbourne, 2003   A. B.

INTRODUCTION

THE AUTHOR

Richard Brinsley Sheridan was born in Ireland in 1751 into a Protestant family of scholars, teachers and writers. His grandfather had been a friend of Swift, who praised him as 'doubtless the best instructor of youth in these kingdoms and perhaps in Europe'.[1] His father, Thomas, compiled a dictionary of pronunciation, wrote and lectured on the art of speaking and was a leading actor in Dublin and London. He was actor-manager of Dublin's Smock Alley Theatre from 1745 until 1754, when a riot led to its destruction. Burdened with debts, Sheridan's parents moved to London, with his elder brother, Charles, and two sisters, leaving their possessions to be auctioned off. In London, Sheridan's mother Frances, urged on by the admiration of Samuel Richardson, published a novel anonymously, *Memoirs of Miss Sidney Bidulph*, and wrote two plays, one, *The Discovery* (1763), a great success. Still pressed hard by their creditors, the family took refuge in France where in 1766 Frances Sheridan died.

Sheridan had left Ireland in 1762 for schooling at Harrow. There, he convinced his teachers that, though idle and apparently learning nothing, he had remarkable abilities. After leaving school, he began to write, and published some translations and light verse. In 1770 the Sheridan family was living in Bath, and there began his dramatic romance with Elizabeth, the beautiful daughter of Thomas Linley the composer, then at the height of her fame as a singer. Pestered by the attentions of an unwelcome suitor, Thomas Mathews, and unhappy that her father expected her to perform frequently in public, where her performances commanded high fees, she accepted help from Sheridan to travel secretly to France with her maid. The plan was for her to stay in a convent known to Sheridan's sisters, to be free from Mathews. At some stage Sheridan declared his love for her, and they were secretly married. When they returned to England Sheridan found that Mathews had slandered him in the Bath newspapers, and he insisted on a duel. They fought, and Sheridan obtained an apology. Soon the disgruntled Mathews was back, eager to fight again. Sheridan met him, and on this occasion was seriously wounded. After some months of separation, and contrary to the wishes of his father, who saw the Linleys as socially inferior, the couple were officially married in 1773. Thomas Linley soon came to accept the situation, but Thomas Sheridan, a man of a difficult temper, remained hostile to his son for many years.

[1] Sichel, I, 218, qtd. in Kelly, p. 3.

Sheridan was determined that his wife should not perform in public. To provide for them he began work on a play, *The Rivals*, performed at Covent Garden in 1775 and followed in the same year by a two-act farce, *St. Patrick's Day*, and by a comic opera, *The Duenna*, the music arranged by his father-in-law. In the following year David Garrick retired after over thirty years as actor and then manager of the Drury Lane Theatre. Sheridan seized this opportunity. With two partners he succeeded in raising funds to buy Garrick's share of the theatre patent, and himself took over the role of manager at Drury Lane. He was then twenty-four. *The School for Scandal* was first performed there in May 1777, and in its first two seasons made £15,000, half of the sum paid to Garrick by the consortium. 1778 saw two spectacular afterpieces, *The Camp*, and *The Critic*, a brilliant theatrical burlesque. *The School for Scandal* and *The Duenna* were to be two of the twelve most performed plays until the end of the century, with *The Critic* the most performed afterpiece. The theatre had given Sheridan fame, and some fortune: he and his elegant wife began to be invited to the homes of the politically influential aristocracy.

Turning away from the stage, Sheridan then set out on a parliamentary career in the Whig party of Fox and Burke. This too made him famous in his day, but drained his finances. He wrote only one more full-length play, *Pizarro*, 1799, an adaptation of a popular tragedy by the German playwright Kotzebue, but continued to play a part in the management of Drury Lane, a connection which left him open to the sneers of his political opponents.[2] In 1780 he was elected member for Stafford, proud to sit 'not as the nominee of any aristocratic patron', but still relying on financial backing from aristocratic friends.[3] His fame as a parliamentarian rests principally on his speeches at the impeachment and trial of Warren Hastings, Governor-General of India, who had been accused of extortion. At the height of his fame, in 1792, Elizabeth died of tuberculosis, leaving a son, Thomas, who was to predecease his father, and an infant daughter, her child by Lord Edward Fitzgerald, whom Sheridan acknowledged as his own, but who died the next year. Three years later he married Esther Ogle, the nineteen-year-old daughter of the Dean of Winchester, a woman given like him to extravagance. They had one child, Charles.

Sheridan was a man of liberal ideas, sympathetic to extending the franchise, and to the American and, initially, French Revolutions. He spoke

---

[2] Lord Holland wrote that at Harrow Sheridan 'was slighted by the master and tormented by the boys, as a poor player's son'. *Further Memoirs of the Whig Party*, (London 1816), p. 240, qtd. in O'Toole, p. 25. Pitt sneered at his 'dramatic turns and his epigrammatic point' as inappropriate in the House, but Sheridan turned the remark back on him. (Kelly, p. 110).

[3] Moore, I, 303.

against the game laws, slavery and discrimination against Catholics. However, his lack of rank or fortune, in a House of Commons full of aristocrats, combined with his determined independence, wit, and rhetorical powers, made his fellow Whigs suspicious of him. His support of the Prince of Wales, and the Prince's reliance on him, further damaged his position with his allies, as, in his later years, did his drinking. Though he remained in parliament for thirty-two years, and was appointed Privy Councillor under Fox in 1806, he was not included in the cabinet, and in the end his political luck, and funds, ran out.

A generous host and friend, he lived when he could in an extravagant, grand style, sustained at other times by his 'confidence in the resources of his own genius'.[4] He failed to keep or answer letters, and under his management the company at Drury Lane complained constantly of not being paid, some in disgust deserting to Covent Garden. On the other hand his capacity to borrow money, and to fund huge schemes, such as the rebuilding of Drury Lane, was remarkable. When the new enlarged theatre burnt down in 1809 it was a major blow. In 1812 he lost his parliamentary seat and, no longer protected by parliamentary immunity from his creditors, was arrested in 1813 for debt. His end followed the pattern of a life marked by contradictions and paradoxes. He died in great poverty, with bailiffs at the door, yet was commemorated with a magnificent funeral with aristocrats as pallbearers. Though he wished to be buried among the politicians his grave in Westminster Abbey is beside Garrick's.

THE PLAY

Sheridan established himself as the leading comic dramatist of the eighteenth century within months of starting to write for the stage. *The Rivals*, first performed on 17 January 1775, initially 'met with a very indifferent reception' and was withdrawn. Eleven days later, with cuts, minor alterations, and one cast change, it returned 'to the warmest bursts of appreciation'.[5] In November of the same year *The Duenna* appeared and took the town by storm. It was a phenomenal success, unequalled since Gay's *The Beggar's Opera* in 1728. Then, late in his first season in management at Drury Lane, on 8 May 1777, his much anticipated new comedy at last appeared: *The School for Scandal*. It too was an immediate success, run-

---

[4] From a satirical essay on his friend by Richard Tickell, qtd. in Moore, II, 228, and Price, p. 20.

[5] *The Monthly Miscellany*, February 1775, *The British Chronicle*, January 27–30, 1775, qtd. in Rhodes, I, 117 and I, 126.

ning for twenty nights, and played forty-five times in the next season. The press hailed him as 'the modern Congreve'.

As if to court comparison with his great predecessors, Sheridan had begun his first season with revivals of Restoration comedies, three by Congreve, 'with alterations', and *A Trip to Scarborough,* a more thoroughly modified version of Vanbrugh's *The Relapse.* No impropriety or 'smuttiness' remained.[6] In his own new play, as in these, language and situations were tempered for audiences who saw themselves as belonging to 'a more polite age'. *The Rivals* appeared in the 1770s when the influence of French 'weeping', or sentimental, comedy made itself felt on the London stage, and when the merits of 'laughing' as against sentimental comedy were in debate. In a prologue to his new play, Sheridan came out against moralizing comedy which moved the audience to tears, and in favour of comedy with humour and wit, but nevertheless 'a heart'. These elements come together in the various strands of *The Rivals. The School for Scandal* attempts an even more ambitious blend. It matches *The Rivals* in comic situations, and in tender feeling, particularly in Charles, the generous-hearted libertine, and in the reconciliation of Sir Peter Teazle and his wife. But here there is also brilliant dialogue, outshining *The Rivals,* and, most tellingly, a satirical edge, a glimpse of human nastiness. The scandalmongers are entertaining but, in comparison to *The Rivals'* amiable fools, malicious: their folly does not quite conceal the damage gossip can cause. There is a chill too about the self-seeking Joseph Surface, as Sheridan's biographer Sichel recognized when characterizing him as 'the Iago of comedy'.[7] The remarkable poise with which Sheridan holds these various elements together has seen the play consistently hailed as the comic masterpiece of the century, standing high with Congreve and Wilde. After its phenomenally successful season, it became one of the first transatlantic successes, being performed in New York on 16 December 1785,[8] with an unauthorized edition appearing in New York (1786) almost as soon as in Dublin (1780). The play can boast a continuous tradition of performance, though it has met with some considerable critical disapproval over the years. This is often precisely on the grounds of its combining comedy of manners with, as Charles Lamb wrote in 1822, 'sentimental

---

[6] Dangle and Sneer in *The Critic* (I.i.147–150) comment on the 'artificial bashfulness' of such politeness. Dangle begins: 'Now, egad, I think the worst alteration is in the nicety of the audience. – No double entendre, no smart innuendo admitted; even Vanbrugh and Congreve obliged to undergo a bungling reformation!'

[7] Sichel, I, 555.

[8] Sichel, I, 581.

incompatibilities'.[9] In the twentieth century the play was thought inferior to Restoration comedy, lacking its sexual frankness. It was seen as tame, conservative, or, worse, sentimental, and dismissed as 'actable and funny'.[10] It is true that Sheridan took over Drury Lane primarily as a speculative investment; he needed a stage success, a play which would make money. He paid attention to his audience, and kept 'politics out of the Theatre', believing that authors who did not were courting danger.[11] But this did not entail a lack of artistic integrity. Sheridan, arguably the only comic dramatist, apart from Shakespeare, who has succeeded in pleasing changing audiences for more than two hundred years, produced in *The School for Scandal* a comedy Shakespearean in range, if differing in its components. Its artificial world of heightened wit and heightened folly amuses its audience; but at times it engages them with moments of human pain and happiness, before delivering them back to its brilliant comedy.

The play in the making

Some of Sheridan's early notes and drafts of the play have survived. They show him at work on two ideas, usually referred to as 'The Slanderers' and 'The Teazles', and perhaps always intended to be combined in one play.[12] The comic situation in 'The Teazles' is that of Wycherley's most famous play, *The Country Wife* (1675). Wycherley's Pinchwife marries Margery from the country and brings her to town, only to find that she is quick to learn its licentious ways. The play, thoroughly purified by Garrick, had been revived as *The Country Girl* in 1766. Sir Peter was at first Old Solomon Teazle, a twice-married man cursing himself, 'O, Blockhead – dolt', for marrying again.[13] His country wife was an outspoken gold-digger: 'having a spirit to spend and enjoy a Fortune I was determined to marry the first Fool I could meet with', she tells him. When he asks: 'Then you wish me dead—' she replies: 'You know I do not—for you have made no settlement on me—'. Her explanation of her taste for wealth was

---

[9] 'On the Artificial Comedy of the Last Century', 1822 and 1823, in *Lamb*, p. 66.

[10] A. N. Kaul, *The Action of English Comedy* (New Haven 1970), p. 137.

[11] *Letters*, III, 220. Sheridan might have been influenced here by his father's disastrous experience in Dublin. See above p. 1. But see John Loftis, 'Political and Social Thought in the Drama' in Hume, pp. 276–7, for Sheridan's veiled attack on the Prime Minister, Lord North, in *The Critic*.

[12] For this view, based on brief references to 'Teazle' material in 'Slanderers' pages, see Redford, p. 9. Certainly the 'Teazle' pages suggest the scandal plot was fitted into the Teazle plot.

[13] All quotations from the sketches follow Redford's transcription.

hardly in keeping with the growing purity of the stage: 'Well Heav'n for-give my mother but I do believe my Father must have been a man of Quality'. On her visit to Young Pliant (i.e. Joseph) she complains of her husband: 'O Hang him—I have told him Plainly that if He continues to be so suspicious I'll leave him entirely and make him allow me a separate Maintenance—'. She even uses the word 'seduced' when mocking her lover's kneeling: 'Nay Nay, I will have no Raptures either— ... if [I] am to be seduced to do wrong—I am not to be taken by Storm'. In the earliest draft of the complete play the couple become more complex and more polite. Sir Peter, now a former bachelor, is a sympathetic figure in part, as Sheridan's first biographer Moore remarked when examining these sketches, because of 'the respectability and amiableness of his sentiments' (I, 231).

'The Slanderers' are early sketches of scandalmongering scenes, and the scheming of the vengeful Lady Sneerwell. Damaged by gossip herself she takes pleasure in damaging others. Her young male confidant devel-oped into the two Surface brothers. To early commentators it appeared that Sheridan modelled Joseph on the sententious hypocrite Malvil in Arthur Murphy's *Know Your Own Mind*,[14] or on Moliere's Tartuffe, a rather less self-conscious hypocrite, and the contrasting brothers who prove in the end to belie their appearances, on Fielding's Tom Jones and Blifil. They also recognized the figure of the wealthy long-lost relative returning in disguise to test his relatives. He had appeared in two recent popular works, one, Sheridan's mother's novel, *Memoirs of Miss Sidney Bidulph* (1756), the other Cumberland's sentimental play, *The West Indian* (1771). Sheridan may have found suggestions for his play in these works, but he could have met them elsewhere. The pairing of brothers, like the old husband with a young wife, is traditional comic material. The ques-tion is always what the dramatist has made of it.

In a review of a production of the play in 1815 Hazlitt nominated two qualities which made *The School for Scandal* 'one of the best comedies in our language': its 'great excellence is in the invention of comic situations, and the lucky contrast of different characters', adding in a footnote: 'The scene where the screen falls and discovers Lady Teazle, is without a rival.'[15] These qualities are of course inseparable, interdependent.

---

[14] Acted at Covent Garden in February 1777, but composed over many years, a first ver-sion rejected by Garrick in 1760.

[15] William Hazlitt, '*The School for Scandal*', *Examiner*, 15 October 1815, *Hazlitt*, p. 61. See also his highly critical account of 'Miss O'Neill's Lady Teazle', pp. 87–8 .

The diversity of the group of scandalmongers provides an obvious illustration of Hazlitt's 'lucky contrast'. Sir Benjamin Backbite is a would-be lover and poet. His uncle Crabtree is pushing his nephew towards the wealthy Maria. The gleeful malice of their gossiping sets off the saccharine false concern of Mrs Candour, a role Jane Austen once read at a country house party, no doubt savouring its comic irony.[16] This trio is quite unaware that their companions, Lady Sneerwell and Joseph, are using gossip for their own ends.

The rest of the major figures, the old bachelor now husband, the flighty wife, the young libertine, the benevolent relative, are recognizable as stock roles, and easily paralleled in contemporary comedies. How far they surpass other versions in interest and appeal is suggested by the various ways actors have performed them. Sir Peter, for instance, may be predominantly comic, irascible, dogmatic, sure he is always right, and now made miserable by his extravagant wife. However, he is warm-hearted in his reconciliation with Charles, and with his wife, and another Sir Peter may quite transcend the bachelor-husband role in his tender longing to enjoy a happy relationship with her. Indeed, this feeling may be felt underlying all their quarrels, and especially their second scene (III.i) which moves with comic inevitablity from good-humoured, loving exchanges into a full-scale row. Lady Teazle, treating her husband rather like an indulgent father, lightheartedly presumes on his affection and is determined to go her own way. Sheridan gives this country wife remarkable depth and ambiguity. When in II.ii she finds Joseph on his knees before Maria and hears his explanation, her response gives a sense of her moral capacities. Joseph may see her as a pupil that he is instructing in the ways of the Town, and she *is* eager to be accepted by Lady Sneerwell's crew; but Joseph does not overwhelm her. She asks wryly 'Do you usually argue on your knees?' Her wariness and command of her situation prepare the audience to accept her final repentance. But in her visit to Joseph (IV.iii) it is impossible to say what would have happened if Sir Peter had not arrived to interrupt them, though a comedy in which she was seduced would not have been acceptable to Sheridan's audience.

The contrast between brothers is also intriguing. Charles is a grateful, generous libertine, no womanizing rake, but loyal to Maria. But his mean, moralizing brother, the self-conscious hypocrite, may be equally engaging, as such actors as Jack Palmer, the original Joseph, or John Gielgud have demonstrated. He is however a more artificial character, with less

[16] See George Holbert Tucker, *Jane Austen the Woman: Some Biographical Insights* (1994), p. 89.

[7]

flesh and blood than Charles. Once defeated, he disappears. Sheridan's father suggested that to invent the pair Sheridan had 'but to dip the pencil in his own heart and he'd find there the characters of both Joseph and Charles.'[17] They are complementary aspects of one personality, in a fashion recalling the double role of Ernest and Jack Worthing in *The Importance of Being Earnest*. A moment revealing an almost twin-like closeness occurs in the last scene when they discover that Sir Oliver is both Premium and Stanley. They need only six words to communicate their recognition that the game is over: 'Charles!', 'Joseph!', ''Tis now complete', 'Very!' (V.iii. 95–8).[18]

For these unusually developed comic figures Sheridan has indeed excelled in inventing comic situations. Many depend on disguise, with Sir Oliver impersonating Mr Premium and Stanley, or concealment, when in IV.iii Sir Peter and Lady Teazle hide. Joseph too is often disguised – as the Man of Sentiment. All these situations give scope for *double entendre*, comically inappropriate remarks, and asides, as in the scene where Sir Oliver as Premium visits Charles. The careful pacing of individual scenes, the placing of their climaxes, and the timing of the introduction of new characters all contribute to the comic effect. Developments are clearly signalled so the audience can either enjoy the suspense, or, when a surprise is sprung on them, grasp what is going on. In Act IV.iii, for instance, the audience knows Joseph is expecting Lady Teazle, and that Sir Peter intends to visit him too, but Charles's arrival is a complete surprise. The various manuscripts of the play provide abundant evidence of Sheridan revising the dialogue before the first performance and for years after, but it appears that he made only one major change to the plot structure: moving the cross-examination of Snake and his confession from III.i to the last scene. As his sister recorded, he had the plotting of the comedy clearly worked out in his mind: 'The comedy is finished; *I have now nothing to do but write it*.'[19]

The throwing down the screen was the great sensation when the play was first performed. It works not only as a brilliant theatrical device; it physically enacts the exposing of truth beneath illusion – a traditional task of comedy. Appropriately, it is the straight talker Charles (named 'Frank' in several pages of the drafts) who insists on the discovery. As a consequence, Lady Teazle, in a moment of self-discovery, acknowledges her

[17] Quoted in Rae, II, 29, note 1.

[18] For the brothers acting 'in concert' see Katharine Worth, *Sheridan and Goldsmith* (Basingstoke 1992), pp. 151–2.

[19] A. Lefanu, *Memoirs of ... Mrs Frances Sheridan* (1824), p. 410, qtd. in Price, p. 290.

feeling for Sir Peter. This falling away of pretence also relates to the unmasking of the brothers' true natures, and, more widely, to the falseness of the social dealings in the play, especially among the scandalmongers. They too are exposed as dealers in falsehood when, much to their surprise, Sir Peter, neither shot through the thorax nor wounded in the side, walks onto the stage. On all levels, with true comic optimism, the play assures its audience the truth will out.

Wit

The most memorable quality of this play is the brilliance of its dialogue. It is, 'from beginning to end', as Moore wrote, 'a continued sparkling of polish and point.'[20] However, he and others after him found fault with Sheridan for sacrificing characterization to repartee. The servant Trip was as witty as his master, and Rowley too had his share of bons mots, notably his remark about Joseph's having 'as much speculative benevolence' as anyone, though 'seldom so sensual as to indulge himself in the exercise of it'(V.i.25–8). But in general the firmness of characterization ensures the play is free of this alleged fault, with the quality varying to suit the character. The scandalmongers' wit, for instance, is appropriately feeble. Their malicious anecdotes amuse *them*, as in the story of Miss Piper's twins, but what the audience find most entertaining is their irrepressible desire to insult their acquaintance. Their victims are usually female. Apart from a glance at young men in debt, their eyes are on women showing off their one good feature, or fat women trying to appear thin. Best of all they relish stories of sexual misdemeanors, of women caught eloping with a servant or attempting to conceal pregnancy. The slant of this gossip reflects the position of a woman in fashionable society where, unless she had a great fortune, nothing, in the Town's view, was more important than her appearance and reputation.

The wit of Sir Peter's and Lady Teazle's 'daily jangles' reaches a higher level. Here, miraculously, jokes about marriage and extravagant wives appear fresh. His complaints are as magnificent as her outrageous replies, her defence of her spending on 'flowers in winter' for example: 'Lord, Sir Peter, am I to blame because flowers are dear in cold weather? You should find fault with the climate and not with me. For my part, I'm sure I wish it was spring all the year round and that roses grew under one's feet!'(II.i.22–5) Such elegantly phrased marital miseries as theirs cannot overwhelm them, nor disturb the audience. Though she has an answer for

20 Moore, I, 247.

everything, their duel of words shows they are well matched in intelligence. What makes the difference is her youthful carelessness, and, on his side, his feeling for her. He has admitted in his first scene: 'Yet ... I doubt I love her, or I should never bear all this.' (I.ii.15–16) In Act IV Lady Teazle will appear to realize that the feeling is mutual. Sentiment breaks down the comic stereotypes of the old man and young wife, and they emerge as an argumentative loving couple to set beside Congreve's Millamant and Mirabell, or Beatrice and Benedict.

In Congreve's plays one must be witty to be admirable. Here it is noticeable that Charles who emerges as the hero is not so much a wit as a plain speaker, or, as Sir Oliver says, 'Exceeding frank ... not a man of many compliments'. (III.iii.122–3) His freedom from conversational hypocrisy itself becomes a kind of wit. He cannot be bothered to pretend to value his ugly family portraits: five pounds will do for great-aunt Deborah as a shepherdess, 'the sheep are worth the money.' (IV.i.44) Aware of his own follies, he has no inclination to be witty at the expense of the follies of others, though he cannot resist mocking 'Morality' (Joseph) and Sir Peter at the fall of the screen: 'there's nothing in the world so noble as a Man of Sentiment!' (IV.iii.376–7) His is a kind of libertine wit which delights in reversing expectations, as in his first line: 'here is the great degeneracy of the age! Many of our acquaintance have taste, spirit, and politeness; but plague on't they won't drink.' (III.iii.1–3) and in refusing to be serious: 'Let me throw on a bottle of champagne, and I never lose—at least I never feel my losses, which is exactly the same thing.' (III.iii.18–19) Joseph too deploys these Wildean phrases but he reverses conventional morality for more sinister purposes. When seducing Lady Teazle, he argues that since a husband should never be deceived, if Sir Peter suspects her, it becomes her 'to be frail in compliment to his discernment.'(IV.iii.55–6) Whether he is intoning moral platitudes or employing casuistry on Lady Teazle, his ingenious hypocrisy is as delightfully shocking as Lady Teazle's outrageousness. From evidence in the drafts of Sheridan's giving a witty line first to one character and then to another John Picker has once again argued that Sheridan cared little for characterization and all for witty effect.[21] But an opposite conclusion is equally possible: that Sheridan moved a witty line around until he found the character it belonged to. If, as I have suggested, the wit is varied to suit the individual roles, it is still the case that the brilliance of the dialogue is pervasive. This quality of the play performs a dramatic function: it har-

---

[21] John M. Picker, 'Disturbing Surfaces: Representations of the Fragment in *The School for Scandal*', *ELH* 65, 3 (1998), 637–52, 639.

monizes the play's comic world, elevates it, and marks it off as an ideally amusing artificial version of fashionable London.

At the same time, the false wit of the scandalmongers is under attack. Sir Peter, Sir Oliver and especially Maria censure those who make clever remarks at others' expense, voicing that mistrust which had appeared earlier in the eighteenth century as a reaction to the 'raillery' of the Restoration man of wit.[22] Lady Sneerwell insists 'there's no possibility of being witty without a little ill nature' (I.i.152–3) but Maria will have none of this. She maintains her opposition to malicious chat and later insists that gossip not motivated by personal resentment is more despicable than that which is.

Scandal and Debt

Sheridan's attraction to the evils of scandal as a literary topic marks him as a man of his time. In a society where the leisured class was small enough for everyone to know everyone, scandalmongering was both enjoyed, and condemned. In Bath, one of the Rules of Conduct affixed by Beau Nash in the Pump Room forbad the repeating of scandal. Sheridan experienced the town's relish of gossip at first hand when events of his own life were bandied about in the papers. His poem 'A Portrait', prefaced to the manuscript of the play he presented to his mistress, Mrs Crewe, addresses the 'prim adepts of scandal's school' and celebrates the lady whose virtue 'casts a gloom o'er scandal's reign'. In an 'Ode to Scandal', published anonymously in 1781, Sheridan again takes a moral view. Here a lady begs Scandal to teach her the art of throwing 'Detraction's dart', but the poem turns when 'Candour' interrupts her, and points to the pathetic figure of a mad 'weeping maid', ruined by the slander of a lover whose base designs she had resisted.

Scandal was not of course a new social evil, or form of entertainment, in the late eighteenth century. But the inclusion of gossip columns in two new journals had made it topical, and opened the gossiping circle to the public at large. *The Morning Post* and the monthly *Town and Country Magazine*, mentioned in Act I, printed scandal, under cover of anonymity, with names suggested by initials.[23] The topic of scandal was not new to the stage either. Wycherley's *The Plain Dealer* (1676) has a scene (II.i) where Olivia, who has just declared her hatred of 'detraction',

---

[22] See Stuart Tave, *The Amiable Humorist* (Chicago 1960), Part I.

[23] Sheridan himself, like Garrick, was not above placing anonymous items in the press to arouse interest in a forthcoming play. For Sheridan later stooping to unsavoury personal scandalmongering, see O'Toole, pp. 382–87.

1. John Neville as Sir Peter Teazle in Peter Wood's 1990 National Theatre production sits surrounded by scandalous newsprint; Zoè Dominic/National Theatre

joins Novel in 'railing' at their acquaintance one by one. Lord Plausible joins them, damning their victims with faint praise. In Congreve's *The Double Dealer* (1694) the ridiculous trio of Lord and Lady Froth and Brisk at the end of the third act laugh at their acquaintance and compete in devising disgusting similes for their defects, while Cynthia, like Sheridan's Maria, comments disapprovingly. In *The Way of the World* (1700) Lady Wishfort and her women friends are said to engage in more harmful forms of scandalmongering:

> last night was one of their cabal-nights; they have 'em three times a week, and meet by turns, at one another's apartments, where they come together like the Coroner's inquest, to sit upon the murdered reputations of the week.
>
> (I.i.)

Other now largely forgotten eighteenth-century comedies had also satirized scandalmongers, notably Dashwould in Murphy's *Know Your Own*

Mind, and Doctor Viper who writes a 'Slanderous Chronicle' in Foote's *The Capuchin* (1776).[24]

In Sheridan's laughing comedy the satire, if it is that, is genial. Scandal is on display rather than under attack. The scandalmongers' ambition is to hold the stage, to be first with the news. This competitiveness makes them more and more ridiculous, culminating in Act V in their elaborate fantasies of a 'duel'. Lady Sneerwell's vengeful plotting with Snake gives scandal a darker shading: as in the best comedy, there is a glimpse of how damage might be done. But whatever the play's title might suggest of their importance, the scandalmongers are ineffective. Lady Teazle's contrite behaviour after the falling of the screen is a response not to them but to her husband's affection and generosity. Sir Peter and Maria, despisers of ill-natured wit, are made anxious by false rumours, but the faithful Rowley ensures that Snake is out-bribed to expose the deceit. With this the threat from scandal disappears, along with Lady Sneerwell, who vanishes like the pantomime wicked fairy, after laying what she intends as a curse on Lady Teazle: 'May your husband live these fifty years!' (V.iii.191–2) a moment which is given a touch of pathos, as Lady Teazle reassures Sir Peter. Rowley's advice to Sir Peter further diminishes the gossips' capacity to expose him, or anyone else, to public ridicule: 'Without affectation, Sir Peter, you may despise the ridicule of fools.' (V.ii.216–17) Thus Sheridan's comic plot proceeds along traditional lines, towards revelations and discoveries, and almost incidentally triumphs over scandal.

The age of scandal was also the age of debt. Debt and money lending are just as much topical issues in the play as scandal. Members of the aristocracy with expensive tastes were able to incur enormous debts thanks to the cooperation of moneylenders, while others, like 'poor Stanley', who had no friends to call on, ended in prison.[25] Charles is a typical rake, extravagant, a gambler, and desperate to borrow. In the scenes with the Jewish broker, Moses, Sir Oliver learns how to impersonate a money lender. Alongside the satirical jabs at the exorbitant interest rates demanded by lenders, there are references to the Annuity Bill passed in the House of Commons in April 1777, and enacted in May, just after the play opened. It attempted to curb the activities of moneylenders, usually

---

[24] See Mark S. Auburn, *Sheridan's Comedies, their Contexts and Achievements* (Lincoln, NE 1977), pp. 135–39, for instances of scandal in eighteenth-century comedy.

[25] Sheridan himself was known for his extravagance, generosity and legendary skill in borrowing money. As a Member of Parliament he was protected from arrest but once out of Parliament he was held for debt.

but not always Jews,[26] by making void contracts with minors, setting up a register of loans, and limiting the annual repayment that could be demanded to half a percent of the sum borrowed, or one pound per £200. Rowley approves of the Bill: 'a young man now must be at years of discretion before he is suffered to ruin himself'. (III.i.113–14)

Sentiment and Sentimental Comedy

While the play's exploration of the pleasures, and risks, of gossip is timeless, some of its other interests are perhaps less easily identified now. Among these are the concepts of sentiment and benevolence, both prominent in eighteenth-century discussions of social behaviour. Sentiment, with the adjective sentimental, recently borrowed from French, denoted then a positive notion: moral or fine feeling, moral sensitivity, or, as often in the play, a remark expressing this feeling. Excessive versions of fine feeling make good comic material, as in the romantic fantasies of Lydia Languish in *The Rivals* and perhaps of Faulkland too, though not everyone agrees he is meant to be ridiculous. In this comedy, however, it is shallow, or worse, *hypocritical,* sentiment that is under attack: the coating of malicious gossip with sweet sentiment, as practised by Mrs Candour, for instance. Fools cannot distinguish true good nature from the pretence, and boast that they can sit for hours hearing 'Lady Stucco talk sentiments.' (II.ii.113) Sheridan was not the first playwright to treat this phenomenon in comedy,[27] but his Joseph is the prince of the sentimental knaves. Though a conscious hypocrite, he is so used to playing the 'Man of Sentiment' that he pretends when there is no need: 'O lud, you are going to be moral ...', 'Egad, that's true' (I.i.109–11). Once Joseph has revealed his true colours in the first scene, Sir Peter's determined enthusiasm for this paragon exposes him to much shrewd comedy.

The play juxtaposes false sentimental feeling and the real thing. True benevolence is seen in action in Charles's generosity, and in Rowley's trust in his goodness. Here the play manifests the influence of early eighteenth-century benevolist thought, grounded on the doctrine of the fundamental goodness of humanity, and the naturalness of the impulse to do

[26] One such was Benjamin Hopkins, the City Chamberlain, who believed he was being attacked in the character of Moses and tried to ban the performance. A Jacob Nathan Moses, who had lent money to one of the part owners of Drury Lane, also feared he was being attacked. See note to III.i.45 and Price, pp. 300–2.

[27] Malvil in Arthur Murphy's *Know Your Own Mind* has some touches of Joseph; he tells Mrs Bromley, a woman who affects tender-heartedness: 'To a person of sentiment, like you, madam, a visit is paid with pleasure.' See *Foote and Murphy,* Act II, p. 184.

good.[28] Prudence becomes, in this context, the antithesis of benevolence, a capacity for cautious, rational thought which restrains the individual from acting on the promptings of the heart. When Charles sends Rowley to take some money to poor Stanley he is generous rather than just. Joseph is untouched by such feelings, while Charles is a stranger to prudence. Sir Oliver's benevolence is genuine, but, as some see it, touched with comic egoism and nostalgia. The old man recognizes his own not 'very prudent' youth in the extravagant Charles, and his exaggerated delight in Charles's affection for him becomes laughable with his repeating 'He would not sell my picture.'

With an elegant structure, brilliant dialogue and warm humanity, the play runs true to the lines in Sheridan's Prologue to the Tenth Night of *The Rivals* which distinguish comedy from 'the goddess of the woeful countenance— / The sentimental muse': it is 'adorned with every graceful art / To charm the fancy and yet reach the heart'. Nevertheless some of its dramatic features do recall characteristics of sentimental comedy. The reformations of Lady Teazle and Charles are in keeping with its exemplary or moralistic turn. Lady Teazle is perhaps on the point of staining her honour when Sir Peter arrives. After her exposure, and her long silence, she denounces Surface, and emerges as a contrite wife. Charles too reforms, presenting himself in the final lines as 'An humbled fugitive from folly' (V.iii.249), who, with Maria as his guide, will presumably abandon drinking, and getting into debt. It is not only Charles's reformation that smacks of sentimental comedy but also his being forgiven for his follies because of the goodness of his heart – his filial affection for Old Noll, and his benevolence to Stanley. Another figure who might appear to step out of sentimental comedy is the virtuous young woman, Maria. In his attack on what he saw as this new form of comedy Goldsmith deplored its replacing of absurd, foolish characters by thoroughly 'good' figures who must 'amuse' the audience with their distresses rather than their follies. Though Maria does shed tears because of her attachment to Charles, her part is not conventional. Early reviewers noted the lack of a scene between her and Charles which would prepare for their move to marriage in the play's last moments. For whatever reason, Sheridan chose not to focus on the romantic aspect of their roles.[29]

---

[28] R. L. Brett, *The Third Earl of Shaftesbury: A Study in Eighteenth-Century Literary Theory* (London 1951), has a valuable discussion of this movement.

[29] One possible reason is the prominence of the romantic element in the Teazle plot. The lack of love scenes has also been attributed to Sheridan's *reshaping* the role to suit Priscilla Hopkins, who replaced Mary Robinson when she declined the part because she was pregnant. Hopkins was judged not to have been a success. However, Christian Deelman (see note 38)

Instead, as noted previously, Maria emerges as a courageous opponent of malicious gossip claiming to be wit. Her firm judgment, and virtual isolation in her social group make her resemble not so much a dramatic figure of sentimental pathos, but a novelistic heroine, a prototype perhaps of Austen's Fanny Price.

The Play and the Critics

The play's reformations, generous feeling and hostility to ridicule mark it as a play of its time. To Lamb its discordant elements, 'a mixture of Congreve with sentimental incompatibilities', were reconciled only by the consummate acting of Jack Palmer as Joseph.[30] Subsequent studies of the development of comedy through the century, with a longer perspective than Lamb's, detect a gradual incorporation of sentimental elements, beginning well before Sheridan, in response to a shift in humour from sharp ridicule to a kindly sympathy with human folly.[31] With another revolution in feeling, these very sentimental elements brought the play into critical disfavour among academic critics in the first half of the twentieth century. Their preference for the unmixed sharp tone of Restoration comedy still survives. However, some contemporary audiences and readers, less quick to equate sentiment with being sentimental (in the negative sense) can enjoy Sir Peter's forlorn moments, and his reconciliation with his wife, in the spirit of romantic comedy. Others take a different view, for the comedy permits this, the fullness of the characterization opening both fine feeling and reformations to question. It is possible to see Sir Oliver's generosity to his nephew as driven by a ridiculous vanity, and to observe that in his reformation speech Charles alludes to reformers' broken promises. Lady Teazle, often taken to be a witty young innocent, may be read as a woman who will yet make Sir Peter discover 'what it is to marry a young wife'. Her reformation does immediately follow Sir Peter's making her a generous allowance. Colman's Epilogue for Lady Teazle begins as a speech of wifely resistance and raises doubts of her settling down in the country. In recent productions, it received strong applause. Sir Peter can say only that he and Lady Teazle '*intend*' to live happily. Though in its last lines Colman has Sheridan urge the moral: 'the fair' should like Lady Teazle abandon folly and play a serious part on the stage of life, in the ending of the play proper morality has a distinctly sub-

---

suggests that the role is as written for Robinson and that Hopkins, for whom it was never intended, was not up to making a success of it.

[30] *Lamb*, p. 66.

[31] On this topic see the works by Robert Hume and Stuart Tave in Further Reading.

dued triumph. Joseph is defeated not by the forces of morality, but, in true comic style, by his own overreaching. He loses control of his plot, and exits, 'his ways unamended.'[32] The scandalmongers will not reform either. Slander and hypocrisy continue to flourish, a situation quite acceptable to the audience since, as Lamb wisely remarked, the artificiality of the comedy permits enjoyment of Joseph's cunning and, indeed, of the scandalmongers' malice.[33] These aspects of the conclusion are in keeping with the intriguing ambiguity of the play's central figures and the complexity of its dramatization of the temptations of life.

STAGING THE PLAY AT DRURY LANE

When Sheridan became manager of Drury Lane in 1776 the theatre was in all essentials as built by Wren in 1674. It was of a size and structure to show off the actor. A new enlarged theatre took its place in 1794, and after the fire of 1807 it was rebuilt on the same scale. These later theatres were 'elephantine', more suited to spectacle than to the psychological acting for which Garrick had been famous. In 1776 the stage still had a forestage in front of the proscenium arch. Much of the acting took place there, close to the audience, in the best lit area. The rest of the space behind the proscenium arch, often known simply as the 'scene', was used mainly for spectacle and mechanical effects. However innovations in lighting introduced by Garrick were changing that. He eliminated the forestage's overhead hoops of candles which had blocked the gallery's sight lines and, following continental practice, introduced on-stage lighting hidden in the wings. A contemporary print of Sheridan's screen scene depicts light slanting in from the side. (See p. 19.) More of the depth of the stage became useable for important dramatic moments, when the actors needed to be well lit. Scenery could now contribute to the effect of realism conjured up by actors on the apron. De Loutherbourg, the designer and painter Garrick had brought to London in 1771, painted two new pieces of scenery especially for this play, one of Charles's picture gallery, (IV.i) with some of the pictures alluded to clearly visible and, for the climactic scene in Joseph's library, an elegant interior with bookcases and a large rear window. It was then not usual to make scenery for each production. Normally stock pieces were employed, all-purpose indoor or outdoor sets of wings and flats, covered with wallpaper, or painted to suggest

---

[32] Christine Wiesenthal, 'Representation and Experimentation in the Major Comedies of Richard Brinsley Sheridan', *Eighteenth-Century Studies*, 25, 3 (1992), 309–30, 327.

[33] *Lamb*, pp. 66–7.

an outdoor scene. The flats, held in grooves fixed on the stage and set at varying distances from the audience, created a larger or smaller acting area. When one pair was set up behind another, a new scene could be revealed when scene-shifters pulled aside those closer to the stage. Drop cloths, recently introduced at Drury Lane, offered an alternative form of scene change.[34]

Early promptbooks list the tables, chairs, glasses, teacups, books, and of course the famous screen, which sparsely furnished the sets. They also note the few hand props, such as a pocket book for Moses, and the 'note' he returns to Trip. Contemporary prints of the fall of the screen show the three male actors dressed as gentlemen in the current fashion, without wigs but with their hair powered white. In Zoffany's portrait of Robert Baddeley as Moses he is wearing an old-fashioned wig, long, curled and unpowdered, marking him as well to do but not a gentleman. (See p. 23.) According to theatrical tradition, Snake was dressed in black, alluding possibly to the clergyman Henry Bate, editor of the *Morning Post*.[35] A costume note in Sheridan's sketches reads: 'Crabtree to wear a Muff'.[36] The elegant Frances Abington (Lady Teazle) was a leader of fashion. When Sheridan took over the management she negotiated a doubling of her annual costume allowance to £120. One reviewer remarked on her 'remarkably low' coiffure, given the current fashion,[37] a nice detail suggesting Lady Teazle's recent arrival in the fashionable world. The auditorium remained lit throughout the performance. The actors could see the audience, and the audience each other. Actors made most of their entrances through the proscenium doors next to the boxes on either side of the stage, and, in contemporary comedies such as this, actors and audience in the adjacent boxes were dressed alike: the stage mirrored the society of the day.

Restoration and eighteenth-century dramatists wrote their plays with particular actors in mind. *The School for Scandal* owed its remarkable success in some degree to Sheridan's shaping the parts so well to the actors' strengths and even, in some cases, to that extension of their usual roles –

[34] These were lowered on a roller; see Colin Visser, 'Scenery and Technical Design', Hume, pp. 92–3.

[35] R. C. Rhodes, *Harlequin Sheridan* (Oxford 1933), pp. 71–2; Bateson suggests the clerical journalist William Jackson, already lampooned by Samuel Foote as Dr Viper in *The Capuchin* (acted 1776), as another 'model' for Snake.

[36] Redford, p. 137.

[37] See Mark S. Auburn, 'Theatre in the Age of Garrick', *S Studies*, p. 26, and note at IV.i.51.

The collapse of the screen, IV. iii, 385. From an original print

2. 'Proscenium of Drury Lane in 1778': the scene in the library at the fall of the screen (IV.iii.364); Victoria & Albert Museum Picture Library

their off-stage personalities.[38] Frances Abington had played both fine ladies and country girls for many years and excelled in this role which subtly combined both. She was at her peak, though at forty only seven years younger than Thomas King, her Sir Peter. Charles was played 'with jovial smartness' by the fine mannered actor, 'Gentleman' William Smith, an old Etonian; Dodd, who played Sir Benjamin, had been a noted Osric and Aguecheek, and was memorably celebrated as 'the prince of pink heels, and the soul of empty eminence'.[39] Philip La Mash, Trip, was the master of gentleman's gentlemen. The triumph was the casting of 'Plausible Jack' Palmer as Joseph. His nickname came from his role of Lord Plausible in *The Plain Dealer*, but it stuck because it fitted him.[40] As theatre manager, Sheridan assigned the actors' roles, and thus was able to assemble a brilliant cast, with established actors playing smaller parts than usual. The result was magnificent. Boaden wrote: 'I think his comedy was better spoken, in all its parts, than any play that I have witnessed on the stage.'[41] Script and performers were ideally suited. Boaden said of King: 'his peculiar sententious manner made him seek and require dialogue of the greatest point.'[42] Frances Abington was just as celebrated in this regard: 'her articulation is so exact, that every syllable she utters is conveyed distinctly, and even harmoniously.'[43] Hazlitt and Lamb, writing forty years later, were convinced that the style of speech and elegance of manners which the play demands had by then been quite lost.

At Drury Lane the performance began with King in costume as Sir Peter speaking Garrick's Prologue. Impersonating the scandal-loving Lady Wormwood, with teacup and newspaper, he transported the audience into the play's world. The green curtain was then drawn up, revealing Lady Sneerwell, sitting at her dressing table alone with Snake. Their conversation introduces the characters, and establishes Joseph's hypocrisy before he appears. Joseph then makes a formal entry, while Maria comes in unannounced, fleeing her suitor and his uncle. But they follow her, and

[38] See the excellent essay by Christian Deelman, 'The Original Cast of *The School for Scandal*', *RES*, N.S. XIII (1962), 257–66.

[39] James Boaden, *Memoirs of the Life of John Philip Kemble*, 2 vols., 1825 (London 1969), I, 55; see also on Dodd, *Lamb*, pp. 56–7 ('On Some of the Old Actors').

[40] Palmer attempted to set up a theatre in rivalry to the patent theatres in 1785, within the Liberty of the Tower; he hung on till 1788 when, forced back to Drury Lane, he finally apologized to Sheridan for attempting to break the patents: 'he is reported to have said, hand on heart, "If you could but see my heart, Mr. Sheridan." The reply was: "Why, Jack, you forget I wrote it!"' (Deelman, p. 258.)

[41] James Boaden, *Memoirs of Mrs Siddons*, 2 vols. (1831), I, 111–12.

[42] Boaden, *Kemble*, I, 59–60.

[43] Davies, II, 175.

one by one the 'school' assembles. Sitting on chairs around the stage they share their gossip, until Maria can bear it no longer and leaves as abruptly as she came.

The next two scenes have fewer characters on stage at once. They were played further down stage, the flats in the first groove, closest to the audience. Sir Peter enters and speaks in soliloquy, one of the means by which this old bachelor husband endears himself to the audience, his informality contrasting with the elaborate compliments of Lady Sneerwell and Joseph. Rowley enters, hears of Sir Peter's disappointment in marriage, and faith in Joseph, announces Sir Oliver's imminent arrival, and the painted act curtain falls. It rises in II.i on the same scenery, and at last Lady Teazle appears, mimicking her husband's dogmatic repetitiveness, their first tiff under way as they enter. She leaves alone to go to Lady Sneerwell's, and Sir Peter, again in soliloquy, confesses his adoration of her even when she is doing everything in her power to 'plague' him.

Flats pulled aside reveal Lady Sneerwell at home to the 'crew'. Another pair of flats with a door in the middle set further back closes off the room. A servant is passing tea, and there are chairs and a card table. When Maria arrives with Lady Teazle, Lady Sneerwell sits her and Joseph down together at cards, possibly right up stage. Lady Teazle remarks on this move to the audience in the first of the play's many asides, a convention widely used at the time, and facilitated by the closeness to the stage of the audience in the pit and lower boxes. When Sir Peter arrives he must be in a convenient position to comment frequently aside as he expresses his disapproval. Lady Sneerwell moves her party into the next room for cards. This long exit up stage through the central door allows, as some manuscripts specify, for conversational pairings as they move off, 'all talking as they are going into the next room'. Sir Peter makes his escape, as Maria had in Act I. Sir Benjamin leads off Lady Teazle, promising to tell her stories of her husband. Joseph, 'Rising with MARIA', tries to press his suit. Maria attempts to leave, but he flings himself at her feet, just as the audience sees Lady Teazle returning through the centre back door. Joseph then sees her: 'Gad's life, here's Lady Teazle', the first of the play's revelations or surprises. Lady Teazle 'comes forward', shoos Maria out, and Joseph launches into an explanation.

The setting of II.iii is another room in Sir Peter's house suitable for intimate serio-comic conversation. The same scenery and characters continue in the next scene, III.i. As with the previous act break, Sheridan has not taken the opportunity to change the scenery, but time has passed. The talk is of the off-stage figure, Stanley, who provides a test of the brothers' benevolence. Also introduced is Moses, 'a friendly Jew'. Sheridan gave

Baddeley, an actor whose special line was foreigners, some lines of broken English, and Baddeley may have introduced others.[44]

The next scene, III.ii, backed by a painted drop cloth of a 'Chamber', moves to Charles's house. It belongs to Trip. After fives lines he leaves '*taking snuff*', in one gesture establishing his pretensions. The drop cloth is raised to discover a Hogarthian scene of a drinking party, a table with a green cloth, chairs, glasses and decanters. Good-humoured talk of drinking, gambling, and toasts to mistresses are followed by a 'Song'. With its four verses, chorus and orchestral accompaniment, it creates a distinctive cheerful effect. Sir Oliver arrives as Mr Premium, and the auction of the family portraits is arranged, with the act break heightening anticipation of the event. The act curtain rises on the picture gallery (partly visible in the Baddeley portrait). On stage is a settee, and 'the gouty chair', an auctioneer's podium for Careless. As the auction ends Charles has the money and Sir Oliver an heir. Sir Oliver, Rowley and Moses then reappear before the III.ii 'Chamber', Moses disapproving of Charles's gift to Stanley: 'Ah, there is the pity of all. He is so damned charitable.' (IV.ii.14) The testing of Charles is complete.

Joseph's library, the second 'new' scene, follows (see p. 19), the large space set with the screen, two chairs and a table. As Joseph waits impatiently for Lady Teazle he orders the servant to adjust the screen. All is ready for a seduction. But he is repeatedly interrupted. As each visitor enters through one of the proscenium doors, Joseph attempts to maintain his various roles. Sir Peter hides in a 'closet', behind the other proscenium door. Charles then arrives. Next Joseph is called away to deal with 'a person', and exits into the wings. Charles, ever forthright, insists on pulling Sir Peter out, and then throws down the screen, revealing Lady Teazle, just as Joseph re-enters. She confesses and leaves. Joseph is still talking 'sentiments' as the act curtain falls.

The final act begins still in the library, with Joseph abusing his servant for admitting 'Stanley'. Rowley announces that Sir Oliver and Charles are on their way. As Joseph waits for them the scene is changed to Sir Peter Teazle's house, and the final appearance of the 'crew' invading the area one by one with their competing versions of the 'duel'. The tattlers are exposed, but irrepressible. As they offer sympathy for his misfortunes, Sir Peter orders them out. Sir Oliver goes off to expose Joseph, and leaves Sir Peter to be reconciled with the weeping Lady Teazle who, though visible to Sir Peter and Rowley, remains off-stage.

The library is revealed again for the last scene. Joseph and Lady Sneerwell are at each other's throats. Sir Oliver as Stanley comes in

44 See note at III.i.94–5.

3. Robert Baddeley as Moses, by Zoffany, with Charles's collection of
pictures in the background; Trustees of the Lady Lever Collection/Walker
Art Gallery

through one door, and Lady Sneerwell retires into the house by the other.
Joseph gives him short shrift and is pushing him out when Charles arrives
and speaks up for Premium. The brothers now both try to push him out

in one of the play's few moments of vigorous action.[45] Sir Peter and Lady Teazle, coming to Joseph's for the first time together, arrive with Maria and Rowley, and identify Sir Oliver. '*After a pause*', the brothers turn '*to each other*', and grasp what has happened. Snake's good deed speeds the denouement until it remains only to bring Maria and Charles together. Charles speaks in verse, heightening the sense of an ending, first to Maria, and then to the audience, telling them their approval can destroy all fears – even of scandal. Mrs Abington spoke Coleman's Epilogue, ending with Sheridan's moral advice to the 'Fair', a piquant moment for those who knew her as the mistress of Lord Shelburne, a liaison recently disclosed in the *Town and Country Magazine*.[46]

RECENT PRODUCTIONS

The School for Scandal has been since its first performance a fixture in the repertoire. It was a favourite with Victorian readers, as well as playgoers, and with the nineteenth-century actor-managers, Sir Henry Irving, Beerbohm Tree, and the Bancrofts, who at the Haymarket introduced a minuet: 'a stately minuet—Mrs Bancroft's happy thought—was danced by Lady Sneerwell's guests', as well as including in the sale of the ancestors 'the banquet scene'.[47] If less elaborately staged, twentieth-century productions were typically glossy and star-studded, such as Olivier's in 1948–9 with costumes by Cecil Beaton, which toured Australia before playing in London, and Gielgud's in 1962, his own performance as Joseph received on Broadway as a model of high comedy acting. In Gielgud's first *School for Scandal* in 1937, the director, Tyrone Guthrie, tried a new approach. He aimed 'to show the itch beneath the powder',[48] focusing on the minor parts, and inventing business for them and the servants. Gielgud triumphed as Joseph but the production was condemned as under-rehearsed. In 1968 Jonathan Miller at the Nottingham Playhouse struck out again in Guthrie's direction, treating the play as 'a work rooted in the rough tangy eighteenth-century world of Hogarth, Smollett and

---

[45] See Laurence Olivier on this lack of movement, and his decision to introduce some 'choreographic moments', in 'On the 1948 Production and Others', in Peter Davison, ed., *Sheridan Comedies: A Casebook* (Basingstoke 1986), p. 154.

[46] See Price, p. 304.

[47] Bancroft qtd. in Rae, II, 320–1. For Charles kissing Uncle Oliver's portrait, and other details of Victorian performances, see the essay by Arthur Colby Sprague listed in Further Reading.

[48] See Gyles Brandreth, *John Gielgud: an Actor's Life* (2000), p. 68.

Fielding'. Actors wore clothes, not elegant costumes, and there was 'no suave wrist work with fans'.[49]

Peter Wood's 1990 production for the National Theatre returned the play to elegance. More than that, it filled the Olivier stage with lavish spectacle. A dumb show of news-sheets being delivered and read preceded the Prologue. The scandalmongers all worked at a large tapestry, stitching up reputations, Sir Oliver was seen disembarking from his ship, and at the beginning of her first scene, Lady Teazle was busy with a dancing lesson. Slanderous tongues and speech ribbons as in Gillray cartoons flew like pennants from the roofs in the set's London skyline. Chairs were upholstered with newsprint. (See p. 12.)

Wood was known as a director of Restoration and eighteenth-century plays who had done away with 'fans and mincing affectation',[50] the despised 'applied' style, and who instead developed the humanity of individual roles. With *The School for Scandal* this was again his approach: as John Neville (Sir Peter) put it, Wood 'humanized' the play.[51] And, in Wood's view, there was great need to do so. As he explained, this was an artificial comedy about an artificial society. So it was to Lamb, but where for Lamb this inspired confidence that the characters could not hurt or be hurt, Wood saw the play as 'very chilly indeed', 'not written affectionately in terms of character'.[52] With the exception of Charles, it lacked, Wood felt, the warm large egos of *The Rivals* (which he had directed in 1983). Wood's Lady Teazle was therefore a young woman innocently engaging in a game of gossip, his Lady Sneerwell not a vengeful fury but a woman driven by desire for Charles. Individual actors were congratulated for 'human', non-caricature, performances, but several reviewers criticized *the play*. It was censured not for being heartless, but for being sentimental, tied by 'contemporary constrictions', weighed down with 'a surfeit of benevolent characters'.[53] Neil Taylor, sensing Wood's interest in 'what Sheridan might be saying about the human heart', accused him of treating the play as a kind of 'dramatized novel', the elaborate settings attempting to create 'a "world" beyond the rooms in which Sheridan's characters have their being'[54] and to give their lives a narrative continuity.

[49] These comments, by Michael Billington, *One Night Stands: a Critic's View of Modern British Theatre* (1993), p. 16, refer to the revival of Miller's production in London, 1972.

[50] Charles Spencer, *Daily Telegraph*, 24 April 1990.

[51] Peter Lewis, 'Unmasking a Masterpiece', *Sunday Times*, 12 April 1990.

[52] 'On Producing Sheridan: A Conversation with Peter Wood', *S Studies*, p. 178, p. 180.

[53] Rhoda Koenig, *Punch*, 4 May 1990; Paul Taylor, *The Independent*, 26 April 1990.

[54] 'City Folk', *TLS*, 4 May 1990.

So for some, in this production at least, the play was wearisomely moral, and for Taylor it was moralized.

Wood in 1995 explained that for him an ideal production should recreate as closely as possible the costumes, manners and grace of the period, and do justice to Sheridan's magnificent rhetoric. But, in an echo of Hazlitt and Lamb, he declared this was now impossible. Actors are not trained for Sheridan's sentences: 'shallow breathing has become the fashion'.[55] In spite of his admiration for the play's dramatic tension and command of comic situation, the play presented a range of problems to him as a director in 1990, not least that he was working in a large theatre, and anxious about his actors being able to entertain the audience by speaking the text.

Declan Donnellan's 1998 Royal Shakespeare Theatre production was in the unglamorous style that, according to Wood, is now in vogue. Its permanent set, the stage open to the back wall with a simple gallery and staircase, was perceived variously as a warehouse, brothel, green room or drinking den. Here the actors, dotted around on the floor or stairs throughout, performed the play for the Prince of Wales, a Sheridan figure at his side. A satirical opening tableau had the Prince centre stage to the singing of Handel's 'See the conquering hero', and a screen falling to reveal the figure of Britannia waggling her trident. Lady Sneerwell, sitting on the Prince's lap, then spoke the Prologue in an Irish accent. This volley of political allusions (amplified by quotations in the programme) gestured towards Sheridan's Irishness, attitudes to the monarchy and the American War of Independence. Once again the production emphasized 'the itch beneath the powder'. Actresses were viewed as prostitutes, the actors bowed elegantly to their Prince, but wore soiled finery; Charles urinated at the back of the stage. Sheridan was at the Prince's side, like Falstaff, hoping to benefit by his noble friend. With its distinctive take on the historical context, the production exuded confidence; much more than Wood's, it had faith in the appeal of the characters, and in the actors' ability to hold the stage speaking the lines. The text was trimmed to eliminate episodes offensive to today's taste, such as making a servant the butt of class comedy. Trip did not appear. The anti-Semitic lines were cut, and, perhaps in a gesture of sympathy for Jewish suffering, Moses was seen being treated more as an outsider than the text suggests. There was no

[55] *S Studies*, p. 180. For one actor's view, see *A World Elsewhere: the Autobiography of Sir Michael Horden with Patricia England* (1993). Horden (Sir Anthony Absolute in Wood's *Rivals*) remarks, p. 152: 'The writing is so convoluted, so intricately built, that if you make one slip it throws you for the next passage. You can't improvise Sheridan.'

laddish song 'Here's to the maiden of bashful fifteen'. Instead Charles and company had women at their drinking party. The chatterers were purposeful rather than affected, with Crabtree greedily eying Maria as a rich prize, and the marriage comedy of Sir Peter and Lady Teazle was played with striking tenderness. In the seduction scene she and Joseph circled round two chairs taking their clothes off piece by piece making explicit the sexual situation implied in their dialogue.[56] Charles's odd habit of lying on the ground in difficult moments implied presumably that an inability to cope lay behind his libertine irresponsibility. This was not perceived as a sentimental production. One reviewer wrote of Charles: 'if he is instantly forgiven by his uncle for refusing to sell his portrait you feel it is more whimsical vanity on the latter's part than a testament to Charles's decency'.[57] Lady Teazle (Emma Fielding) was delicately ambiguous: not yet 'a natural' when competing at Lady Sneerwell's, while to another reviewer, 'a slippery Irish beauty quick to deny any responsibility for near-seduction by Joseph Surface'.[58] In the screen scene, the performances did justice to the play's range, 'combining farce, witty cynicism and pathos in almost equal measure',[59] Sir Peter 'an irrational despot whose awakening to his wife's potential infidelity is tragic'. Overall, the production was seen to rescue 'the play from cosmetic prettiness' and to treat 'it illuminatingly as a barbed comment on a divided Georgian society'.[60] However, not all knew what to make of the politicizing frame. Sheridan's biography had been brought into play but to what end? Nevertheless, the vitality of the production was greeted with applause. And it deserved it, if only for its solution to the vexed issue of 'style'. The manners, movement, and clothes of the eighteenth-century actors gathered around the Prince were carried over with ease and grace into their roles in the play proper. And no newspaper critic complained that the actors could not do justice to Sheridan's wit.

A Note on the Text

The copy text of this edition is the Tickell MS, a fair copy of the play owned by Elizabeth Ann Tickell. 'Betsy', the daughter of one of Sheridan's closest friends, Richard Tickell, (d. 1790) and of Mary, née Linley,

---

[56] Moves repeated in the Sydney Theatre Company's 2000 production.

[57] *Guardian*, 15 October 1998.

[58] Jeremy Kingston, *Times*, 16 October 1998; *Guardian*, 15 October 1998.

[59] Viv Thomas, *Stratford upon Avon Herald*, 15 October 1998.

[60] *Guardian*, 15 October 1998.

4. Joseph Surface (Jason O'Mara) and Lady Teazle (Emma Fielding), in Declan Donnellan's 1998 RST production, begin to take their clothes off (IV.iii); Malcolm Davis/Shakespeare Centre Library

(d. 1787), was Sheridan's niece by marriage. After her mother's death, the Sheridans took her into their family and she was present at Elisabeth's death. Another uncle, also married to a Linley sister, the playwright Charles W. Ward, was secretary to the Board of Managers of Drury Lane Theatre from September 1808. Thus, though, as Price notes, there is no proof connecting this MS with a 'playhouse copy', at that time Elizabeth Tickell had theatre associations which may explain how she came by a copy of the promptbook.[61] The inclusion in the MS of Sheridan's poem 'A Portrait', once prefixed to a copy presented to Mrs Crewe, suggested to Bateson that the copy derived from a family source rather than from Drury Lane. Elizabeth Tickell was of course in a position to benefit from both. After his own extensive researches on the MSS, and drawing on the work of the editor of the standard edition, Cecil Price, Bateson became convinced that Tickell was the latest version to record revisions by Sheridan, and thus preferred it over those earlier MSS in which Sheridan's hand had been identified making corrections, and which form the basis of Price's eclectic text. Tickell and other 'Manuscripts not inscribed by Sheridan' are relegated by Price (I, 341) to an inferior category.

---

[61] 1808 is also the date of the watermark of the MS.

As Price himself recognized, the 'real importance' of the Tickell MS lies in its closeness to the first authorized edition of the play, published by Murray in 1821. Bateson put this more firmly: this was the MS that 'authenticated' Murray. Murray's edition had been disparaged by Moore, the first biographer, and, Bateson notes, 'even the judicious Price refuses to accept its authority' (p. xlix). Tickell and Murray share some unique readings; however in the few readings where they differ, Bateson almost always prefers Tickell as the version free from the later editorial correction or modernizing, which, for example, replaces 'miserablest' with 'most miserable' (I.ii.3). This edition therefore follows Tickell, with modernized spelling and punctuation. In comparison to Sheridan's own writing and the earlier MSS, Tickell MS punctuation is closer to modern conventions, making use of commas, semi-colons and stops as well as the dash.

In one important respect this edition differs from the previous New Mermaid. Bateson saw it as the task of an editor to print not just the latest, but what he judged to be the best revisions, 'the best of Sheridan's text' (p. lv). He therefore produced his own eclectic text, and on occasions printed variants from earlier MSS, the 1799 Dublin edition, or Murray's, when in his judgment these were 'better readings' than Tickell's. In a number of cases, Tickell readings rejected by Bateson are here restored. In short, this edition, though in most details following the text produced by Bateson, moves slightly closer to Tickell, leaving its readings to stand, as a record of Sheridan's latest revisions. Any exceptions are discussed in the notes.

Sheridan did not allow The School for Scandal to be printed in his lifetime. The phenomenal popularity of the play, combined with the lack of an authorized published text, resulted in actors putting together texts for acting, and publishers, especially in Dublin, producing many pirated editions. Sheridan was repeatedly involved in negotiations with printers, but no edition appeared. To one impatient publisher, Ridgeway, Sheridan quipped: 'The fact is, Mr R., I have been nineteen years endeavouring to satisfy my own taste in this play, and have not yet succeeded.'[62] He worked sporadically on the text, refining and polishing it. The results, what Price called 'a multitude of minor alterations of phrasing', are preserved in various MSS. Five MSS of the whole play antedate Tickell, a group referred to in the footnotes as 'MSS'. These are the Frampton Court MS, a long version in Sheridan's handwriting; the MS presented to the Lord Chamberlain for licensing; and three post-performance presentation MSS. By far the greatest dissimilarity among these MSS is between

---

[62] Thomas Moore, Memoirs, Journal and Correspondence 2 vols. (1853–6), II, 302, qtd. in Price, p. 329.

Frampton Court and the rest. Passages cut from it are printed in full in Price's edition. Numerous later variants appear in the incomplete MS Spunge, with Tickell recording Sheridan's last improvements. Many of the variants after the first performance text are minor: singulars replace plurals, or vice versa, 'Oh' replaces 'Ah', 'it's' replaces 'it is'. Readers who wish to examine the full collation are referred to Price's edition and to Bateson's review of the variants in his.

Collation entries in the notes here are concerned principally with readings where Tickell and Murray differ from the earlier MSS more substantially than in reading 'would not' instead of 'wouldn't'. Most differences noted are either slight shifts or refinements of meaning, or small cuts. For example: *to outwit* replaces 'to endeavour to outwit', *dear friend* 'good friend' and *Egad* 'That's droll, egad'. A few are more significant and substantial. In addition, comparisons are made with the Spunge MS, though its revisions, mostly in Act I, were apparently largely forgotten, or rejected. A second major concern is to note all variants between Tickell and Murray, where Tickell may reasonably be thought to preserve Sheridan's last effort before London publishers and editors at last got their hands on the manuscript after his death. The aim is to make this late version available to readers and performers, who may then make their own choice between its readings and Sheridan's earlier ideas.

In comparison to the earlier MSS, the Tickell MS has fewer stage directions or *Asides*. The presentation copies have most, many in Sheridan's hand. Given their authority, and interest to readers and performers, stage directions from the earlier MSS have been included in the text, with their origin identified in the footnotes. Information about stage business and settings from early Drury Lane promptbooks is also included in the notes. Stage directions supplied by the Editor are placed in square brackets.

ABBREVIATIONS

F Court	Frampton Court MS, the earliest surviving version, in Sheridan's hand (Princeton)
Lord C	MS submitted to the Lord Chamberlain for Licencing, May 1777 (Yale)
Buck	post first performance MS belonging to Albinia, Countess of Buckinghamshire
Crewe B	post first performance MS belonging to Mrs Crewe, with many revisions and stage directions in Sheridan's hand
Georgetown	post first performance MS inscribed to Mrs Crewe, with many revisions (Georgetown University)
MSS	F Court, Lord C, Buckingham, Crewe B, Georgetown, the group of five complete MSS in Sheridan's hand or with autograph revisions. When a variant occurs in *only one of the group* the collation note will read, for e.g. *scandalous* Tickell, MSS (slanderous F Court).
Spunge	incomplete MS with many alterations in Sheridan's hand 'perhaps c. 1787' (Bateson) (British Library)
Powell	MS copy of the promptbook of Act I.i and most of I.ii. c. 1809 (Harvard Theatre Collection, Houghton Library)
Tickell	MS post 1808 owned by Elizabeth Ann Tickell (Bodleian Library)
Scott	MS promptbook (Harvard Theatre Collection, Houghton Library)
1779	MS promptbook Acts II–IV dated Portsmouth, 1779, an early unauthorized version (Harvard Theatre Collection, Houghton Library)

PUBLICATIONS

Bateson	F. W. Bateson ed., *The School for Scandal*, The New Mermaids (1979), 2nd ed., with an article by David Crane (1995)
Crane	David Crane ed., Richard Brinsley Sheridan, *The Critic*, The New Mermaids (1989)
Davies	Thomas Davies, *Memoirs of the Life of David Garrick* (1780), ed. Stephen Jones, 1808, 2 vols. (New York 1969)
Dublin 1780	*The School for Scandal*, 1780. A Facsimile (Menston, Yorkshire 1969)
ELH	*English Literary History*
F and M	George Taylor ed., *Plays by Samuel Foote and Arthur Murphy* (Cambridge 1984)
Frances Sheridan	Robert Hogan and Jerry C. Beasley, eds., *The Plays of Frances Sheridan* (Newark 1984)
Hazlitt	*Hazlitt on Theatre*, William Archer and Robert Lowe eds., 1895 (New York 1959)
Hume	Robert H. Hume, ed., *The London Theatre World 1660–1800* (Carbondale 1980)
Johnson's *Dictionary*	Samuel Johnson, *A Dictionary of the English Language*, 1755 (Hildesheim 1968)
Kelly	Linda Kelly, *Richard Brinsley Sheridan. A Life* (1997).
Lamb	Roy Park, ed., *Lamb as Critic*, The Routledge Critics Series (London and Henley 1980)
Letters	*The Letters of Richard Brinsley Sheridan*, ed. Cecil Price, 3 vols. (Oxford 1966)
Moore	Thomas Moore, *Memoirs of the Life of the Right Honourable Richard Brinsley Sheridan*, 2 vols., 2nd ed. (1825)
Murray	Richard Brinsley Sheridan, *Works* (1821)
N & Q	*Notes and Queries*

OED	*Oxford English Dictionary*
O'Toole	Fintan O'Toole, *A Traitor's Kiss: the Life of Richard Brinsley Sheridan* (1997)
Price	Cecil Price ed., *The Dramatic Works of Richard Brinsley Sheridan,* 2 vols. (Oxford 1973)
Redford	Bruce Redford, ed., *The Origins of 'The School for Scandal'* (Princeton 1986)
Rae	W. Fraser Rae, *Sheridan: A Biography,* 2 vols. (1896)
RES	*Review of English Studies*
Rhodes	R. Crompton Rhodes ed., *The Plays and Poems of Richard Brinsley Sheridan,* 3 vols. (New York 1962)
S Studies	James Morwood and David Crane, eds., *Sheridan Studies* (Cambridge 1995)
Sichel	Walter Sichel, *Sheridan,* 2 vols. (1909)
TLS	*Times Literary Supplement*

OTHER ABBREVIATIONS

ed.	editorial emendation
qtd.	quoted
s.d.	stage direction
s.p.	speech prefix

FURTHER READING

EDITIONS

A. Norman Jeffares, ed., *The School for Scandal* (1967)

Cecil Price, ed., *The Dramatic Works of Richard Brinsley Sheridan*, 2 vols. (Oxford 1973)

F. W. Bateson, ed., *The School for Scandal*, The New Mermaids (1975), 2nd ed., with an article by David Crane (1995)

Michael Cordner, ed., *The School for Scandal and Other Plays*, Oxford English Drama (Oxford 1998)

STAGING

Christian Deelman, 'The Original Cast of *The School for Scandal*', *RES*, N.S. XIII (1962) 257–66

C. B. Hogan, ed., *The London Stage Part 5 1776-1800*, (Carbondale 1968)

Philip H. Highfill Jr. et al., *A Biographical Dictionary of Actors, Actresses, Musicians, Dancers, Managers and Other Stage Personnel in London, 1660-1800* (Carbondale 1973–93)

Robert D. Hume, ed., *The London Theatre World 1660–1800* (Carbondale 1980)

Tiffany Stern, *Rehearsal from Shakespeare to Sheridan* (Oxford 2000)

CRITICAL STUDIES

Arthur Sherbo, *English Sentimental Drama* (East Lancing, MI 1957)

Stuart Tave, *The Amiable Humorist* (Chicago 1960)

Arthur Colby Sprague, 'In Defence of a Masterpiece: *The School for Scandal* Re-examined', *English Studies Today*, third series, ed. G. Duthie (Edinburgh, 1964) 125–36

Robert D. Hume, 'Goldsmith and Sheridan and the supposed revolution of "Laughing" against "Sentimental" Comedy', *Studies in Change and Revolution Aspects of English Intellectual history 1640–1800* (Menston, Yorkshire 1972) pp. 237–76, reprinted in Robert D. Hume, *The Rakish Stage* (Carbondale 1983)

John Loftis, *Sheridan and the Drama of Georgian England* (Oxford 1976)

Mark S. Auburn, *Sheridan's Comedies: their Contexts and Achievements* (Lincoln, Nebraska, 1977)

James Morwood, *The Life and Works of Richard Brinsley Sheridan* (Edinburgh 1985)

Patricia Meyer Spacks, *Gossip* (New York 1985). Chapter 6 discusses comedies of scandal.

Peter Davison, ed., *Sheridan Comedies: a Casebook* (Basingstoke 1986)

Robert Hogan, 'Plot, Character, and Comic Language in Sheridan', in A. R. Braunmuller and J. C. Bulman eds., *Comedy from Shakespeare to Sheridan: Change and Continuity in the English and European Dramatic Tradition*, Essays in Honour of Eugene M. Waith (Newark 1986) pp. 274–85

Bruce Redford, ed., *The Origins of 'The School for Scandal'* (Princeton 1986)

Brown, Marshall, *Preromanticism* (Stanford 1991). Chapter 9 discusses 'Sheridan's Semiotics'.

Christine S. Wiesenthal, 'Representation and Experimentation in the Major Comedies of Richard Brinsley Sheridan', *Eighteenth-Century Studies*, 25, 3 (1992) 309–30

Katharine Worth, *Sheridan and Goldsmith* (Basingstoke 1992)

James Morwood and David Crane, eds., *Sheridan Studies* (Cambridge 1995)

Alexander Leggatt, *English Stage Comedy 1490–1990* (1998)

John M. Picker, 'Disturbing Surfaces: Representations of the Fragment in *The School for Scandal*', *ELH*, 65, 3 (1998) 637–52

The title page of the Tickell MS
*Reproduced with the permission of the Bodleian Library,
the University of Oxford*

The School for Scandal a form of title for a comedy familiar since Molière's *L'École des Femmes* (1662). Compare, for example, Arthur Murphy's *The School for Guardians* (1767) and Hugh Kelly's *The School for Wives* (1773).
Right Honourable The title of a Privy Councillor: Sheridan became a member of the Privy Council in 1806.

THE

SCHOOL FOR SCANDAL

COMEDY

In Five Acts

By

The Right Honourable

Richard Brinsley Sheridan.

PROLOGUE

Written by D. Garrick, Esqr.

Spoken by Mr King

A School for Scandal! Tell me, I beseech you,
Needs there a school this modish art to teach you?
No need of lessons now, the knowing think;
We might as well be taught to eat and drink.
Caused by a dearth of scandal, should the vapours   5
Distress our fair ones—let them read the papers.
Their powerful mixtures such disorders hit;
Crave what they will—there's *quantum sufficit.*
'Lord!' cries my Lady Wormwood (who loves tattle,
And puts much salt and pepper in her prattle),   10
Just risen at noon, all night at cards when threshing,
Strong tea and scandal—'Bless me how refreshing!
Give me the papers, Lisp—how bold and free! (*sips*)
Last night Lord L. (sips) was caught with Lady D.
For aching heads what charming *sal volatile!* (*sips*)   15
If Mrs B. will still continue flirting,
We hope she'll draw, or we'll undraw the curtain.
Fine satire, poz—in public all abuse it,
But, by ourselves, (*sips*) our praise we can't refuse it.
Now, Lisp, read you—there, at that dash and star.'   20
'Yes, ma'am: *A certain lord had best beware,*

Written ... Esqr. Georgetown, Buck, both in Sheridan's hand. David Garrick (1717–79),
actor, playwright and from 1747–76 manager of Drury Lane Theatre
Spoken ... King Georgetown (spoken by Mr Garrick   Tickell). A curious slip. Thomas
King (1730-1805) was the original Sir Peter Teazle, and an actor frequently asked to
deliver prologues.
5 *vapours* common expression for low spirits, fainting, etc., especially in women, once
thought to be produced by internal 'exhalations'
8 *quantum sufficit* Latin for a sufficient amount, the phrase used in medical prescriptions
11 *threshing* figuratively, beating, belabouring, as in threshing corn
13 s.d. *sips* King presumably carried a cup of tea and a newspaper
14 *Lord L.* The form in which newspapers gossip columns named their victims; compare
V.ii.214.
15 *sal volatile* smelling salts, an antidote to the 'vapours'
18 *poz* positively; feminine slang; cf. II.ii.1, II.ii.46.

Who lives not twenty miles from Grosvenor Square;
For should he Lady W. find willing,
Wormwood is bitter'—'Oh! That's me, the villain!
Throw it behind the fire and never more   25
Let that vile paper come within my door.'
Thus at our friends we laugh, who feel the dart;
To reach our feelings, we ourselves must smart.
Is our young bard so young to think that he
Can stop the full spring-tide of calumny?   30
Knows he the world so little, and its trade?
Alas, the devil's sooner raised than laid.
So strong, so swift, the monster there's no gagging.
Cut Scandal's head off, still the tongue is wagging.
Proud of your smiles once lavishly bestowed,   35
Again our young Don Quixote takes the road;
To show his gratitude he draws his pen
And seeks this hydra Scandal in his den.
For your applause, all perils he would through—
He'll fight—that's write—a cavalliero true,   40
Till every drop of blood—that's ink—is spilt for you.

22 *Grosvenor Square* one of the exclusive elegant residential areas built west of the City in
    the later seventeenth and eighteenth centuries
24 *Wormwood* bitter tasting plant (*artemisia absinthium*), one of several names in the play
    associating bitterness with scandalmongers
29 *our young bard* At the first performance, Sheridan was 25.
35 *Proud ... bestowed* Alluding to the popularity of *The Rivals* and *The Duenna* (both per-
    formed in 1775).
36 *Don Quixote* Likening Sheridan's war on scandal to the chivalric, deluded exploits of
    the Spanish knight ('cavalliero', l. 40).
38 *hydra* in classical mythology, a monster with many heads, destroyed by Hercules After
    den Lord C, Crewe B, Buck and other Prologue MSS insert: From his fell gripe the
    frighted fair to save / Tho he should fall—th'attempt must please the brave.

DRAMATIS PERSONAE

[and Original Cast]

Men

Sir Peter Teazle	Mr King
Sir Oliver Surface	Mr Yates
Joseph Surface	Mr Palmer
Charles Surface	Mr Smith
Crabtree	Mr Parsons
Sir Benjamin Backbite	Mr Dodd
Rowley	Mr Aickin
Moses	Mr Baddeley
Trip	Mr La Mash
Snake	Mr Packer
Careless	Mr Farren
Sir Harry	Mr Gaudry
Companions to Charles, Servants	

Women

Lady Teazle	Mrs Abington
Maria	Miss P. Hopkins
Lady Sneerwell	Miss Sherry
Mrs Candour	Miss Pope
Maid	Mrs Smith

From the Tickell MS

THE SCHOOL FOR SCANDAL

Act I, Scene i

LADY SNEERWELL's *house*
Discovered LADY SNEERWELL *at the dressing table;* SNAKE *drinking chocolate*

LADY SNEERWELL

The paragraphs, you say, Mr Snake, were all inserted?

SNAKE

They were, madam, and as I copied them myself in a feigned hand, there can be no suspicion whence they came.

LADY SNEERWELL

Did you circulate the report of Lady Brittle's intrigue with Captain Boastall? 5

SNAKE

That's in as fine a train as your ladyship could wish. In the common course of things I think it must reach Mrs Clackitt's ears within four and twenty hours—and then, you know, the business is as good as done.

LADY SNEERWELL

Why truly Mrs Clackitt has a very pretty talent—and a great 10 deal of industry.

SNAKE

True, madam, and has been tolerably successful in her day. To my knowledge she has been the cause of six matches being

---

o s.d. 2 LADY SNEERWELL A Lady Sneerwell appears in Henry Fielding's satirical comedy *Pasquin* (1736).

at the Dressing table Dressing-room scenes are common in Restoration and eighteenth-century comedies, e.g. Lady Wishfort's in Congreve's *The Way of the World* (III.i).

SNAKE In the early drafts the confidant is Spatter, then Miss Verjuice, a poor female relation. Snake, previously an off-stage figure only, replaced her in a last minute alteration, as is revealed by changes to speech prefixes in the manuscript submitted for licensing (Lord C). Lady Sneerwell and Snake are 'discovered', i.e. on stage when the curtain rises.

o s.d. 3 *chocolate* the fashionable morning drink

1 *paragraphs* items of libellous gossip appearing in newspapers such as the notorious *Morning Post* (founded 1772)

4 *intrigue* clandestine liaison

7 *Clackitt* In Johnson's *Dictionary* 'to clack' is 'to let the tongue run', and in Frances Sheridan's play *The Dupe* the talkative Mrs Friendly is spoken of as 'Madam Clack'.

broken off and three sons being disinherited, of four forced elopements, as many close confinements, nine separate maintenances, and two divorces. Nay, I have more than once traced her causing a *tête-à-tête* in the *Town and Country Magazine*, when the parties perhaps had never seen each other's face before in the course of their lives. 15

LADY SNEERWELL

She certainly has talents, but her manner is gross. 20

SNAKE

'Tis very true. She generally designs well, has a free tongue, and a bold invention; but her colouring is too dark and her outlines often extravagant. She wants that delicacy of hint and mellowness of sneer which distinguishes your ladyship's scandal.

LADY SNEERWELL

Ah, you are partial, Snake. 25

SNAKE

Not in the least. Everybody allows that Lady Sneerwell can do more with a word or a look than many can with the most laboured detail, even when they happen to have a little truth on their side to support it.

They rise

LADY SNEERWELL

Yes, my dear Snake, and I am no hypocrite to deny the satisfaction I reap from the success of my efforts. Wounded myself in the early part of my life by the envenomed tongue of slander, I confess I have since known no pleasure equal to the reducing others to the level of my own injured reputation. 30

SNAKE

Nothing can be more natural. But, Lady Sneerwell, there is one 35

---

17 *tête-à-tête* the title under which an item of scandal regularly appeared in the monthly *Town and Country Magazine* (founded 1769), with the couple concerned identified by initials or pseudonyms, and with a plate showing their portraits in vignette

18–19 *each other's face* Tickell, Murray (each other's faces   MSS). A variant 'typical' of these versions' 'greater linguistic precision' (Bateson).

21–4 *designs ... mellowness* Playing on terms used in the criticism of drawing.

29 s.d. *They rise* Spunge in Sheridan's hand. Their sitting alone, without even a maid, establishes their complicity. A maid, Lappet, appears only in the earliest MS, F Court, and is sent off at *family* l. 39.

32–3 *envenomed tongue of slander* Compare 'The Slanderers', title of Sheridan's original satirical scenes of scandal-mongers (see Redford; Moore and Price include some extracts).

affair in which you have lately employed me wherein, I confess, I am at a loss to guess your motives.

LADY SNEERWELL

I conceive you mean with respect to my neighbour Sir Peter Teazle and his family?

SNAKE

I do. Here are two young men, to whom Sir Peter has acted as a   40
kind of guardian since their father's death—the eldest possessing the most amiable character and universally well spoken of, the youngest the most dissipated and extravagant young fellow in the kingdom, without friends or character—the former an avowed admirer of your ladyship and apparently   45
your favourite; the latter attached to Maria, Sir Peter's ward— and confessedly beloved by her. Now, on the face of these circumstances, it is utterly unaccountable to me why you, the widow of a City knight, with a good jointure, should not close with the passion of a man of such character and expectations as   50
Mr Surface—and more so, why you should be so uncommonly earnest to destroy the mutual attachment subsisting between his brother Charles and Maria.

LADY SNEERWELL

Then at once to unravel this mystery, I must inform you that love has no share whatever in the intercourse between Mr   55
Surface and me.

SNAKE

No!

LADY SNEERWELL

His real attachment is to Maria—or her fortune. But finding in

---

41 *eldest* Tickell, MSS (elder   Georgetown, Spunge)

43 *youngest* Tickell, MSS (other   Spunge)

46 *attached to* i.e. emotionally attached to, in love with; compare Charles: 'you know my attachment to Maria' (IV.iii.278).

48 *circumstances* Spunge inserts: circumstances which I'm sure I state fairly

49 *widow . . . jointure* Spunge replaces this with: widow, your own mistress, and independent in your fortune
    City knight City (i.e. London) merchant who had been knighted, with an implied social inferiority to a rural land-holding knight
    jointure money a husband undertakes at the time of the marriage to bequeath to his wife

50 *passion* Tickell, MSS, Murray (addresses   Spunge in Sheridan's hand). A more polite term, but compare II.ii.199.

55 *intercourse* dealings, without any sexual connotation

his brother a favoured rival he has been obliged to mask his
pretensions and profit by my assistance.   60

SNAKE

Yet still I am more puzzled why you should interest yourself in
his success.

LADY SNEERWELL

How dull you are! Cannot you surmise the weakness which I
hitherto through shame have concealed even from you? Must I
confess that Charles, that libertine, that extravagant, that   65
bankrupt in fortune and reputation, that he it is for whom I am
thus anxious and malicious—and to gain whom I would
sacrifice everything?

SNAKE

Now, indeed, your conduct appears consistent; but how came
you and Mr Surface so confidential?   70

LADY SNEERWELL

For our mutual interest. I have found him out a long time
since. I know him to be artful, selfish, and malicious—in short,
a sentimental knave, while with Sir Peter, and indeed with all
his acquaintance, he passes for a youthful miracle of prudence,
good sense, and benevolence.   75

SNAKE

Yes, yet Sir Peter vows he has not his equal in England; and
above all, he praises him as a Man of Sentiment.

---

63 *How dull you are!* Tickell, Murray (Heavens! how dull you are! MSS, Spunge,
   Powell). A change dictated by 'the need for an ever greater moral delicacy of
   expression' (Price, p. 348), or to be consistent with her 'glacial self-control' (Bateson).
64 *you? Must* Spunge inserts: you? Where is the sagacity that should have almost anticipated my own consciousness of my weakness? Must
73 *sentimental* in a favourable sense, 'exhibiting refined and elevated feeling' (*OED*, 1),
   'given to moral reflections' (Price); from 'sentiment' in the sense of refined, tender
   emotion; emotional reflection or meditation, e.g. ll. 106–8; see Surface's cynical use of
   this sense, l. 111. Because his refined feeling is only a pretence he is indeed a 'sentimental knave'. See p. 14.
73–5 *while ... benevolence* Tickell, Lord C, Crewe B, Buck, Powell (not in Georgetown)
76 *Yes, yet Sir Peter* Tickell, Powell, Murray (Yes, yes, I know   Lord C; Yet   Spunge,
   Georgetown; Yes, I know him   Crewe B). A much revised passage with the Tickell version neatly pointing to the two views of Joseph.
77 *Man of Sentiment* a popular eighteenth-century form of play title, e.g. *The Man of Taste*
   (1735), *The Man of Quality* (1773), and also Henry McKenzie's highly successful novel
   The Man of Feeling (1771).

LADY SNEERWELL

True; and with the assistance of his sentiments and hypocrisy
he has brought him entirely into his interest with regard to
Maria, while poor Charles has no friend in the house, though I   80
fear he has a powerful one in Maria's heart, against whom we
must direct our schemes.

Enter SERVANT

SERVANT

Mr Surface.

LADY SNEERWELL

Show him up.

Exit SERVANT

Enter [JOSEPH] SURFACE

SURFACE

My dear Lady Sneerwell, how do you do today? Mr Snake, your   85
most obedient.

LADY SNEERWELL

Snake has just been arraigning me on our mutual attachment; but
I have informed him of our real views. You know how useful he
has been to us, and, believe me, the confidence is not ill placed.

---

78 *sentiments* Tickell, MSS (sentiment   Murray). See II.ii.113 for further evidence of 'sen-
    timents' (expressions of fine feeling) and 'sentiment' (fine feeling) being in this period
    virtually interchangeable.

79 *him* i.e. Sir Peter Tickell, MSS (Sir Peter   F Court, Bateson)

80–2 *while poor ... schemes* Tickell, MSS (not in Georgetown).

84 *him up.* Tickell, Murray (him up. He generally calls about this time. I don't wonder at
    people's giving him to me for a lover. *Exit* MSS, Powell). The omission may be due
    to the Tickell copyist having reached the bottom of the page (Bateson), or another
    instance of the 'ever greater need for moral delicacy'; see l. 63n. Nothing further is
    made of the rumour of an intrigue between these two, despite possible opportunities
    later (see note at IV.iii.324).

84 s.d. *Exit* SERVANT MSS except F Court, Powell (not in Tickell). Tickell usually omits *exit*
    when a servant is sent away.
    s.d. 2 SURFACE Tickell, MSS; Joseph's title as the elder son, used throughout for speech
    prefixes; Mrs Surface is an ingratiating landlady in Frances Sheridan's play *A Trip to
    Bath*.

87 *arraigning* Tickell (rallying   Murray). Bateson suggests Murray here is following the
    1780 'Dublin' edition.

SURFACE

Madam, it is impossible for me to suspect a man of Mr Snake's 90
sensibility and discernment.

LADY SNEERWELL

Well, well, no compliments now; but tell me when you saw
your mistress, Maria—or what is more material to me, your
brother.

SURFACE

I have not seen either since I left you; but I can inform you that 95
they never meet. Some of your stories have taken a good effect
on Maria.

LADY SNEERWELL

Ah, my dear Snake, the merit of this belongs to you. But do
your brother's distresses increase?

SURFACE

Every hour. I am told he has had another execution in the 100
house yesterday. In short, his dissipation and extravagance
exceed anything I have ever heard of.

LADY SNEERWELL

Poor Charles!

SURFACE

True, Madam, notwithstanding his vices, one can't help feeling
for him. Aye, poor Charles! I'm sure I wish it were in my power 105
to be of any essential service to him, for the man who does not
share in the distresses of a brother, even though merited by his
own misconduct, deserves—

LADY SNEERWELL

O lud, you are going to be moral, and forget that you are
among friends. 110

SURFACE

Egad that's true. I'll keep that sentiment till I see Sir Peter.
However, it certainly is a charity to rescue Maria from such a
libertine, who, if he is to be reclaimed, can be so only by a

---

91 *discernment* Tickell, MSS (discernment and general— Spunge)

99 *distresses* 'Distress' is a legal term for the seizure of goods in place of the payment of a
debt.

100 *execution* the execution of a court order for the seizure of a debtor's goods

109 *O lud* O Lord, a 'minced', i.e. affectedly refined, form of the oath
be moral For Surface, this means making moralizing remarks.

111 *Egad* a polite form of 'by God'
that's true. I'll Tickell, MSS (Egad, that's true—so I was indeed. I'll Spunge)

person of your ladyship's superior accomplishments and
understanding.   115

SNAKE

I believe, Lady Sneerwell, here's company coming. I'll go and
copy the letter I mentioned to you. Mr Surface, your most
obedient.

SURFACE

Sir, your very devoted.

Exit SNAKE

Lady Sneerwell, I am very sorry you have put any further   120
confidence in that fellow.

LADY SNEERWELL

Why so?

SURFACE

I have lately detected him in frequent conference with old
Rowley, who was formerly my father's steward and has never,
you know, been a friend of mine.   125

LADY SNEERWELL

And do you think he would betray us?

SURFACE

Nothing more likely. Take my word for't, Lady Sneerwell, that
fellow hasn't virtue enough to be faithful even to his own
villainy. Hah, Maria!

Enter MARIA

LADY SNEERWELL

Maria, my dear, how do you do? What's the matter?   130

MARIA

Oh, there is that disagreeable lover of mine, Sir Benjamin
Backbite, has just called at my guardian's with his odious Uncle
Crabtree. So I slipped out, and ran hither to avoid them.

---

119 *very devoted* Tickell, MSS (very devoted and most faithful   Spunge). A theatrically
  effective addition, given what Surface goes on to say.

129 *Hah, Maria!* An unannounced, and agitated entry: 'What's the matter?', l. 130, and '...
  ran hither', l. 133.

131 *lover* Here referring to a despised suitor, but elsewhere to a more intimate admirer; see
  note at I.i.84.

133 *Crabtree* Crab-apples being proverbially sour, his name suggests sourness of disposition, and tongue (as do Verjuice, Lady Sneerwell's original female confidante, and
  Wormwood in the Prologue).
  slipped out, and ran Tickell, MSS (made my escape and have run   Spunge)

LADY SNEERWELL

Is that all?

SURFACE

If my brother Charles had been of the party, ma'am, perhaps   135
you would not have been so much alarmed.

LADY SNEERWELL

Nay, now you are severe; for I dare swear the truth of the
matter is, Maria heard *you* were here. But, my dear, what has
Sir Benjamin done that you should avoid him so?

MARIA

Oh, he has done nothing; but 'tis for what he has said. His   140
conversation is a perpetual libel on all his acquaintance.

SURFACE

Aye, and the worst of it is there is no advantage in not knowing
him, for he'll abuse a stranger just as soon as his best friend—
and his uncle's as bad.

LADY SNEERWELL

Nay, but we should make allowance. Sir Benjamin is a wit and   145
a poet.

MARIA

For my part, I confess, Madam, wit loses its respect with me
when I see it in company with malice. What do you think, Mr
Surface?

SURFACE

Certainly, Madam. To smile at the jest which plants a thorn in   150
another's breast is to become a principal in the mischief.

LADY SNEERWELL

Pshaw, there's no possibility of being witty without a little ill
nature. The malice of a good thing is the barb that makes it
stick. What's your opinion, Mr Surface?

---

137 *severe* Tickell, MSS (ill-natured   Spunge in Sheridan's hand). 'Joseph is unkind rather
than censorious' (Bateson).

141 *libel* correctly, slander; cited in *OED* as an example of popular use

147 *confess* Tickell (own   MSS). Maria underlines her conviction with an ironic apology.

152 *Pshaw* post-Restoration expression of contempt or disgust

153 *a good thing* here, a witty remark

[48]

SURFACE

To be sure, Madam, that conversation where the spirit of   155
raillery is suppressed will ever appear tedious and insipid.

MARIA

Well, I'll not debate how far scandal may be allowable; but in a
man, I am sure, it is always contemptible. We have pride, envy,
rivalship, and a thousand motives to depreciate each other; but
the male slanderer must have the cowardice of a woman before   160
he can traduce one.

Enter SERVANT

SERVANT

Madam, Mrs Candour is below and, if your ladyship's at
leisure, will leave her carriage.

LADY SNEERWELL

Beg her to walk in.

[*Exit* SERVANT]

Now, Maria, however, here is a character to your taste, for   165
though Mrs Candour is a little talkative, everybody allows her
to be the best-natured and best sort of woman.

MARIA

Yes, with a very gross affectation of good nature and benevolence,
she does more mischief than the direct malice of old Crabtree.

SURFACE

I'faith that's true, Lady Sneerwell. Whenever I hear the current   170
running against the characters of my friends, I never think them
in such danger as when Candour undertakes their defence.

---

155 *To be sure* Tickell, MSS (Certainly   F Court; Undoubtedly   Spunge). To avoid repe-
tition of 'Certainly', l. 150.

156 *raillery* 'good-humoured ridicule, banter' *OED*, but in this context more sharp and
malicious, as suggested by 'thorn', 'barb', 'stick'

157 s.p. *MARIA* Tickell (LADY SNEERWELL   MSS). Perhaps a copyist's error.

157–61 *Well, I'll not debate . . . traduce one* Refusing to debate further the propriety of 'scandal',
Maria (or Lady Sneerwell) insists that male slanderers are contemptible. Both sexes
have 'a thousand motives' to disparage each other, but a man who defames a woman
by malicious gossip is imitating women's cowardly tactics. Underlying the remark is
the double standard, which viewed the moral behaviour of women more severely than
that of men. Damage to a woman's 'reputation' was irreparable.

163 *will leave her carriage* i.e. to visit Lady Sneerwell

164 *Beg her to walk in* Tickell, MSS (I shall be happy to see her   Spunge). An idle variation.

166 *Candour* openness, freedom from malice, here in a newer, ironic sense, implying
malice passed off as frankness; compare 'Save, save, oh, save me from the Candid
Friend' (Canning, 'The New Morality', *The Anti-Jacobin*, 1798; *OED* 'candid' 5b).

LADY SNEERWELL
Hush! Here she is.

Enter MRS CANDOUR

MRS CANDOUR
My dear Lady Sneerwell, how have you been this century? Mr
Surface, what news do you hear? Though indeed it is no matter,   175
for I think one hears nothing else but scandal.

SURFACE
Just so, indeed, ma'am.

MRS CANDOUR
Ah, Maria, child! What, is the whole affair off between you and
Charles? His extravagance, I presume? The town talks of
nothing else.   180

MARIA
I am very sorry, ma'am, the town has so little to do.

MRS CANDOUR
True, true, child; but there's no stopping people's tongues. I
own I was hurt to hear it, as indeed I was to learn from the
same quarter that your guardian, Sir Peter, and Lady Teazle
have not agreed lately as well as could be wished.   185

MARIA
'Tis strangely impertinent for people to busy themselves so.

MRS CANDOUR
Very true, child, but what's to be done? People will talk; there's
no preventing it. Why, it was but yesterday I was told that Miss
Gadabout had eloped with Sir Filigree Flirt. But Lord, there's
no minding what one hears—though to be sure I had this from   190
very good authority.

MARIA
Such reports are highly scandalous.

MRS CANDOUR
So they are child—shameful, shameful! But the world is so
censorious, no character escapes. Lord, now who would have
suspected your friend Miss Prim of an indiscretion? Yet such is   195
the ill nature of people that they say her uncle stopped her last

179 *The town* usual expression for the fashionable society of London
181 *has so little to do* Tickell, MSS (is not better employed   Spunge)

week just as she was stepping into the York diligence with her dancing-master.

MARIA

I'll answer for't there are no grounds for that report.

MRS CANDOUR

Oh, no foundation in the world, I dare swear. No more probably than for the story circulated last month of Mrs Festino's affair with Colonel Cassino—though to be sure that matter was never rightly cleared up.

SURFACE

The licence of invention some people take is monstrous indeed.

MARIA

'Tis so—but in my opinion those who report such things are equally culpable.

MRS CANDOUR

To be sure they are. Tale-bearers are as bad as the tale-makers—'tis an old observation, and a very true one. But what's to be done, as I said before? How will you prevent people from talking? Today Mrs Clackitt assured me Mr and Mrs Honeymoon were at last become mere man and wife like the rest of their acquaintance. She likewise hinted that a certain widow in the next street had got rid of her dropsy and recovered her shape in a most surprising manner. And at the same time Miss Tattle, who was by, affirmed that Lord Buffalo had discovered his lady at a house of no extraordinary fame— and that Sir Harry Bouquet and Tom Saunter were to measure swords on a similar provocation. But, Lord, do you think I would report these things? No, no, tale-bearers, as I said before, are just as bad as the tale-makers.

SURFACE

Ah, Mrs Candour, if everybody had your forbearance and good nature.

---

197 *diligence* fast stage-coach
202 *Festino* like 'conversazione', l. 247, a currently fashionable Italian term for an entertain-
       ment; compare 'Subscription Festinos', Italianate entertainments advertized in 1776
       (Price, p. 365).
       Cassino a card game
215 *Buffalo* Alluding to the horns of the cuckold.
216 *of no extraordinary fame* of ill repute
217 *Harry Bouquet* also a character in Sheridan's 'musical entertainment' *The Camp*, 1778;
       for *bouquets* see note at III.ii.26.

MRS CANDOUR

I confess, Mr Surface, I cannot bear to hear people attacked
behind their backs, and when ugly circumstances come out
against one's acquaintance, I own I always love to think the   225
best. By the bye, I hope 'tis not true that your brother is
absolutely ruined?

SURFACE

I am afraid his circumstances are very bad indeed, ma'am.

MRS CANDOUR

Ah, I heard so—but you must tell him to keep up his spirits.
Everybody almost is in the same way—Lord Spindle, Sir   230
Thomas Splint, Captain Quinze, and Mr Nickit. All up, I hear,
within this week. So if Charles is undone, he'll find half his
acquaintance ruined too, and that, you know, is a consolation.

SURFACE

Doubtless, ma'am, a very great one.

Enter SERVANT

SERVANT

Mr Crabtree and Sir Benjamin Backbite.   *Exit*   235

LADY SNEERWELL

So, Maria, you see your lover pursues you; positively you shan't
escape.

[*Enter* CRABTREE *and* SIR BENJAMIN BACKBITE]

CRABTREE

Lady Sneerwell, I kiss your hands. Mrs Candour, I don't believe
you are acquainted with my nephew, Sir Benjamin Backbite?
Egad! ma'am, he has a pretty wit—and is a pretty poet too, isn't   240
he, Lady Sneerwell?

SIR BENJAMIN

Oh, fie, Uncle!

230–1 *Spindle, Splint* Suggesting gentlemen whose fortunes are broken, patched together, or
thin, lacking robustness.
231 *Quinze, Nickit* Identifying these two as gamblers: *Quinze* a card game where the winner
holds cards closest to fifteen; *nick* a winning throw at dice.
Nickit Tickell, MSS (*Pharo*   Spunge). Another gambling card game.
232–3 *his acquaintance* Tickell, MSS (his friends and acquaintance   Spunge)
235 s.d. *Exit* (*Exit* SERVANT   Georgetown, Powell, not in Tickell)

CRABTREE

Nay, egad, it's true. I back him at a rebus or a charade against
the best rhymer in the kingdom. Has your ladyship heard the
epigram he wrote last week on Lady Frizzle's feather catching   245
fire? Do, Benjamin, repeat it—or the charade you made last
night extempore at Mrs Drowzie's conversazione. Come now:
your first is the name of a fish, your second a great naval
commander, and—

SIR BENJAMIN

Uncle, now, prithee—   250

CRABTREE

I'faith, ma'am, 'twould surprise you to hear how ready he is at
all these fine things.

LADY SNEERWELL

I wonder, Sir Benjamin, you never publish anything.

SIR BENJAMIN

To say truth, ma'am, 'tis very vulgar to print. And as my little
productions are mostly satires and lampoons on particular   255
people, I find they circulate more by giving copies in
confidence to the friends of the parties. However, I have some
love elegies, which, when favoured with this lady's smiles, I
mean to give the public.

CRABTREE

'Fore Heaven, ma'am, they'll immortalize you. You will be   260

243 *rebus or a charade* forms of riddle where each syllable of the word or words is suggested
     by a pun, picture, or cryptic clue, as in Mr Elton's rhymed 'courtship' riddle in
     Austen's *Emma* vol. I, ch. ix.
247 *conversazione* Italian term adopted in the eighteenth century for a private social gath-
     ering for music and 'elegant discourse on cultural topics' (Bateson)
251-2 *at all these fine things* Tickell (at these things   MSS; at all these fine sort of things
     Murray)
254 *'tis very vulgar to print* Congreve disgusted Voltaire 'by the despicable foppery of desir-
     ing to be considered not as an author, but as a gentleman', S. Johnson, 'Congreve',
     Lives of the Poets. Though Bateson thought Backbite 'out of date with his convenient
     excuse', the attitude persisted. Thomas Grey was reported to have 'had a Quixotic
     notion that it was beneath a gentleman to take money from a bookseller'; see H. M.
     Paull, *Literary Ethics* (London 1928), p. 329. For evidence of Sheridan's believing that
     gentlemen did not put their poems before the public, see '*Ode to Scandal*' *together with
     'A Portrait' by R. B. Sheridan,* ed. R. Compton Rhodes (1927), p. 31, and Rhodes, III,
     359–60. Sheridan claimed he had authorized only two publications in his lifetime, a
     political pamphlet and *The Duenna.* (Price, p. 5)
258 *love elegies* i.e. love poems

handed down to posterity, like Petrarch's Laura, or Waller's Sacharissa.

SIR BENJAMIN

Yes, madam, I think you will like them when you shall see them on a beautiful quarto page, where a neat rivulet of text shall meander through a meadow of margin. 'Fore Gad, they will be the most elegant things of their kind. 265

CRABTREE

But, ladies, that's true. Have you heard the news?

MRS CANDOUR

What, sir, do you mean the report of—

CRABTREE

No, ma'am, that's not it. Miss Nicely is going to be married to her own footman! 270

MRS CANDOUR

Impossible!

CRABTREE

Ask Sir Benjamin.

SIR BENJAMIN

'Tis very true, ma'am. Everything is fixed and the wedding livery bespoke.

CRABTREE

Yes, and they do say there were pressing reasons for't. 275

LADY SNEERWELL

Why, I have heard something of this before.

MRS CANDOUR

It can't be. And I wonder anyone should believe such a story of so prudent a lady as Miss Nicely.

SIR BENJAMIN

O lud, ma'am, that's the very reason 'twas believed at once. She

261 *Petrarch's Laura* lady addressed in the poems of Petrarch (Francesco Petrarca, 1304–74)

261–2 *Waller's Sacharissa* lady addressed in the poems of Edmund Waller (1606–87), a poet admired by a previous generation for his smooth verses. Millamant and Mirabell in Congreve's *The Way of the World* (1700) quote him (IV.i and ii). 'The conjunction of Petrarch and Waller was a Grub Street commonplace.' (Bateson)

265 *meander* Tickell, Murray (murmur MSS, Powell). Even more appropriate, given that Backbite's greatest interest is in how his poems will look.

266 *kind* Tickell, MSS (species Spunge)

273–4 *wedding livery* suits of clothes, uniforms, for servants to wear at the wedding

275 *pressing* urgent, also a sexual innuendo, suggesting intercourse

279 *that's the very ... She* Tickell, MSS (you have mentioned the very circumstances that made it believed at once. Yes, she Spunge)

has always been so cautious and so reserved that everybody was   280
sure there was some reason for it at bottom.

MRS CANDOUR

Why, to be sure, a tale of scandal is as fatal to the credit of a
prudent lady of her stamp as a fever is generally to those of the
strongest constitutions. But there is a sort of puny, sickly
reputation that is always ailing, yet will outlive the robuster   285
characters of a hundred prudes.

SIR BENJAMIN

True, madam, there are valetudinarians in reputation as well as
in constitution, who, being conscious of their weak part, avoid
the least breath of air and supply their want of stamina by care
and circumspection.   290

MRS CANDOUR

Well, but this may be all a mistake. You know, Sir Benjamin, very
trifling circumstances often give rise to the most injurious tales.

CRABTREE

That they do, I'll be sworn, ma'am. Did you ever hear how
Miss Piper came to lose her lover and her character last
summer at Tunbridge? Sir Benjamin, you remember it?   295

SIR BENJAMIN

Oh, to be sure—the most whimsical circumstance.

LADY SNEERWELL

How was it, pray?

CRABTREE

Why, one evening at Mrs Ponto's assembly the conversation
happened to turn on the breeding Nova Scotia sheep in this
country. Says a young lady in company, 'I have known   300
instances of it, for Miss Letitia Piper, a first cousin of mine, had
a Nova Scotia sheep that produced her twins'. 'What,' cries the
Lady Dowager Dundizzy (who you know is as deaf as a post)
'has Miss Piper had twins?' This mistake, as you may imagine,

---

295   *Tunbridge* watering place outstripped by Bath in the eighteenth century; Crabtree,
Bateson remarks, is once again behind the times.

298   *Ponto* the ace of trumps in the game quadrille; another allusion to fashionable society's
passion for cards.

299   *breeding* Tickell, Murray (difficulty of breeding   MSS, Powell). In 'The Slanderers'
Miss Piper is 'Miss Shepherd of Ramsgate', but Sheridan sacrificed the puns. *The Rivals*
had been criticized for puns and 'shameful absurdities in language' (qtd. in Rhodes, I,
124). England held the (formerly French) colony of Nova Scotia throughout the eighteenth century.

threw the whole company into a fit of laughter. However, 'twas   305
next morning everywhere reported—and in a few days believed
by the whole town—that Miss Letitia Piper had actually been
brought to bed of a fine boy and a girl. And in less than a week
there were some people who could name the father and the
farm-house where the babies were put to nurse.   310

LADY SNEERWELL

Strange indeed!

CRABTREE

Matter of fact, I assure you. O lud, Mr Surface, pray is it true
that your uncle Sir Oliver is coming home?

SURFACE

Not that I know of, indeed, sir.

CRABTREE

He has been in the East Indies a long time. You can scarcely   315
remember him, I believe? Sad comfort, whenever he returns, to
hear how your brother has gone on.

SURFACE

Charles has been imprudent, sir, to be sure; but I hope no busy
people have already prejudiced Sir Oliver against him. He may
reform.   320

SIR BENJAMIN

To be sure, he may. For my part I never believed him to be so
utterly void of principle as people say, and, though he has lost
all his friends, I am told nobody is better spoken of by the Jews.

CRABTREE

That's true, egad, nephew. If the Old Jewry was a ward, I
believe Charles would be an alderman. No man more popular   325
there, 'fore Gad! I hear he pays as many annuities as the Irish

---

315 *East Indies* at this time understood to include the Indian subcontinent

323 *the Jews* i.e. moneylenders, though later it is clear that Christians are also moneylenders (III.i.76.)

324 *Old Jewry* street in the City of London where Jews lived and had a synagogue before
their expulsion from England in 1291, and after their readmittance under Cromwell
ward division of a city electing an alderman to the city council

326 *annuities* here, interest paid annually on a loan

tontine—and that whenever he is sick they have prayers for the recovery of his health in the Synagogue.

SIR BENJAMIN

Yet no man lives in greater splendour. They tell me when he entertains his friends he can sit down to dinner with a dozen of his own securities, have a score of tradesmen waiting in the antechamber, and an officer behind every guest's chair. 330

SURFACE

This may be entertainment to you, gentlemen, but you pay very little regard to the feelings of a brother.

MARIA

Their malice is intolerable. Lady Sneerwell, I must wish you a good morning. I'm not very well. *Exit* 335

MRS CANDOUR

Oh dear, she changes colour very much.

LADY SNEERWELL

Do, Mrs Candour, follow her: she may want assistance.

MRS CANDOUR

That I will, with all my soul, ma'am. Poor dear girl, who knows what her situation may be. *Exit* 340

LADY SNEERWELL

'Twas nothing but that she could not bear to hear Charles reflected on, notwithstanding their difference.

SIR BENJAMIN

The young lady's penchant is obvious.

CRABTREE

But, Benjamin, you must not give up the pursuit for that.— Follow her, and put her into good humour. Repeat her some of your own verses. Come, I'll assist you. 345

SIR BENJAMIN

Mr Surface, I did not mean to hurt you; but depend on't your brother is utterly undone.

326–7 *Irish tontine* A form of lottery (invented by Lorenzo Tonti) to raise a loan in which lenders were paid a lifetime annuity, the amount increasing with the death of each lender. Eighteenth-century Irish and English parliaments raised funds in this way.

328 *the Synagogue* Tickell, MSS (all the Synagogues Murray). There was only one in London until the early nineteenth century.

331 *securities* those who have undertaken to secure his loans

332 *officer* bailiff. Sir Benjamin mocks Charles by pretending all the various debt collectors in Charles's house are the numerous guests and servants of someone living in great style.

CRABTREE

O lud, aye ! Undone as ever man was. Can't raise a guinea!

SIR BENJAMIN

And everything sold, I'm told, that was moveable.   350

CRABTREE

I have seen one that was at his house. Not a thing left but some empty bottles that were overlooked—and the family pictures, which I believe are framed in the wainscots.

SIR BENJAMIN

And I'm very sorry, also, to hear some bad stories against him.

Going

CRABTREE

Oh, he has done many mean things, that's certain.   355

SIR BENJAMIN

But, however, as he's your brother—   *Going*

CRABTREE

We'll tell you all another opportunity.

Exit CRABTREE *and* SIR BENJAMIN

LADY SNEERWELL

Ha, ha! 'Tis very hard for them to leave a subject they have not quite run down.

SURFACE

And I believe the abuse was no more acceptable to your   360
ladyship than Maria.

LADY SNEERWELL

I doubt her affections are farther engaged than we imagined. But the family are to be here this evening, so you may as well dine where you are, and we shall have an opportunity of observing farther. In the meantime, I'll go and plot mischief—   365
and you shall study sentiments.

Exeunt

---

353   *wainscots* wooden panelling
354   s.d. *Going* Tickell (and at l. 356). Other MSS insert *Going* more or less often (six times in Georgetown) with Spunge alternating *Going* and *Returns*; all suggest comic business whereby nephew and uncle make repeated half-exits and returns.
358–9   *not quite run down* not quite finished off, as in hunted down and killed
361   *Maria* Tickell, MSS (to Maria   Georgetown)
362   *I doubt* I fear; compare I.ii.16.
366   *sentiments* Tickell, MSS (sentiment   Murray); moral aphorisms.

Act I, Scene ii

SIR PETER [TEAZLE]'s *house*
Enter SIR PETER [TEAZLE]

SIR PETER

When an old bachelor marries a young wife, what is he to
expect? 'Tis now six months since Lady Teazle made me the
happiest of men—and I have been the miserablest dog since we
committed matrimony. We tiffed a little going to church, and
came to a quarrel before the bells were done ringing. I was   5
more than once nearly choked with gall during the honeymoon,
and had lost all comfort in life before my friends had done
wishing me joy. Yet I chose with caution—a girl bred wholly in
the country, who never knew luxury beyond one silk gown, nor
dissipation above the annual gala of a race ball. Yet now she   10
plays her part in all the extravagant fopperies of the fashion and
the town, with as ready a grace as if she had never seen a bush
nor a grass plat out of Grosvenor Square. I am sneered at by all
my acquaintance and paragraphed in the newspapers. She
dissipates my fortune and contradicts all my humours. Yet the   15
worst of it is, I doubt I love her, or I should never bear all this.
However, I'll never be weak enough to own it.

Enter ROWLEY

  0 s.d. *SIR PETER [TEAZLE]'s house* The form of phrase identifying scene settings varies
       throughout Tickell. Compare II.iii.0 s.d., III.ii.0 s.d., etc.
  1 *old bachelor* here and elsewhere (e.g. II.iii.3) recalling Congreve's comedy *The Old
       Bachelor*, revived by Sheridan at Drury Lane (November 1776)
       marries Tickell, Murray (takes   MSS)
  3 *miserablest* Tickell, MSS (most miserable   Murray)
3–4 *since ... matrimony* Tickell (that ever committed wedlock   F Court, Georgetown; the
       phrase added, then deleted, Spunge; ever since   other MSS). Bateson omits, finding
       Sir Peter's humorous variant on 'committed murder' uncharacteristic.
  4 *tiffed* had a slight disagreement, or tiff
  5 *came to a quarrel* Tickell, MSS (fairly quarrelled   Murray)
  6 *gall* feeling of bitterness, rancour, traditionally associated with the bitter fluid secreted
       by the gall-bladder
 13 *plat* plot (a now obsolete variant)
       Grosvenor Square another reference to the fashionable West End residential area; com-
       pare Prologue l. 22.
 14 *paragraphed* mentioned in a newspaper paragraph, in the style of the Prologue ll. 14–24
 15 *dissipates* fritters away

ROWLEY

Oh, Sir Peter, your servant. How is it with you, sir?

SIR PETER

Very bad, Master Rowley, very bad. I meet with nothing but
crosses and vexations.   20

ROWLEY

What can have happened to trouble you since yesterday?

SIR PETER

A good question to a married man!

ROWLEY

Nay, I am sure your lady, Sir Peter, can't be the cause of your
uneasiness.

SIR PETER

Why, has anybody told you she was dead?   25

ROWLEY

Come, come, Sir Peter, you love her, notwithstanding your
tempers don't exactly agree.

SIR PETER

But the fault is entirely hers, Master Rowley, I am myself the
sweetest-tempered man alive and hate a teasing temper—and
so I tell her a hundred times a day.   30

ROWLEY

Indeed!

SIR PETER

Aye—and what is very extraordinary in all our disputes she is
always in the wrong. But Lady Sneerwell and the set she meets
at her house encourage the perverseness of her disposition.
Then, to complete my vexations, Maria, my ward, whom I   35
ought to have the power of a father over, is determined to turn
rebel too, and absolutely refuses the man whom I have long
resolved on for her husband;—meaning, I suppose, to bestow
herself on his profligate brother.

ROWLEY

You know, Sir Peter, I have always taken the liberty to differ 40
with you on the subject of these two young gentlemen. I only
wish you may not be deceived in your opinion of the elder. For
Charles (my life on't!), he will retrieve his errors yet. Their

---

19 *Master* Sir Peter and Sir Oliver Surface, both older men, use this respectful form of
address for a valued retainer.

29 *teasing* annoying, irritating

worthy father, once my honoured master, was at his years
nearly as wild a spark; yet, when he died, he did not leave a   45
more benevolent heart to lament his loss. ·

SIR PETER

You are wrong, Master Rowley. On their father's death, you
know, I acted as a kind of guardian to them both, till their uncle,
Sir Oliver's, eastern liberality gave them an early independence.
Of course, no person could have more opportunities of judging   50
of their hearts, and I was never mistaken in my life. Joseph is
indeed a model for the young men of the age. He is a Man of
Sentiment, and acts up to the sentiments he professes; but for
the other, take my word for't, if he had any grain of virtue by
descent, he has dissipated it with the rest of his inheritance. Ah,   55
my old friend Sir Oliver will be deeply mortified when he finds
how part of his bounty has been misapplied.

ROWLEY

I am sorry to find you so violent against the young man,
because this may be the most critical period of his fortune. I
came hither with news that will surprise you.   60

SIR PETER

What? Let me hear.

ROWLEY

Sir Oliver *is* arrived and at this moment in town.

SIR PETER

How? You astonish me. I thought you did not expect him this
month.

ROWLEY

I did not; but his passage has been remarkably quick.   65

45 *spark* 'A lively, splendid, showy gay man. It is commonly used in contempt' (Johnson's
   Dictionary). Rowley is indulgent rather than contemptuous.
46 *benevolent heart* benevolence, charitable feeling, highly esteemed in the eighteenth century as leading to active goodness; Joseph has a reputation for benevolence (I.i.75); see
   pp. 14–15.
47 *wrong Master Rowley* Tickell, MSS, Murray (wrong Master Rowley, you are wrong
   Spunge). An amusing addition to Sir Peter's insistent repetitions; compare l. 19, and see
   ll. 51 and 75 for further Spunge additions.
49 *eastern liberality* MSS, Powell, Scott (liberality   Tickell). Derived from money-making
   in the 'East Indies' (I.i.315); apparently an accidental omission in Tickell.
51 *life* Tickell, MSS (life, that much I may say   Spunge)
52–3 *Man of Sentiment* Sir Peter confirms the account of his admiration for Joseph's integrity, I.i.73–7.

SIR PETER

Egad, I shall rejoice to see my old friend. 'Tis fifteen years since we met. We have had many a day together. But does he still enjoin us not to inform his nephews of his arrival?

ROWLEY

Most strictly. He means, before it is known, to make some trial of their dispositions.   70

SIR PETER

Ah, there needs no art to discover their merits; however, he shall have his way. But pray, does he know I am married?

ROWLEY

Yes, and will soon wish you joy.

SIR PETER

What, as we drink health to a friend in a consumption? Ah, Oliver will laugh at me. We used to rail at matrimony together,   75 and he has been steady to his text. Well, he must be soon at my house, though. I'll instantly give orders for his reception. But, Master Rowley, don't drop a word that Lady Teazle and I ever disagree.

ROWLEY

By no means.   80

SIR PETER

For I should never be able to stand Noll's jokes. So I'd have him think, Lord forgive me, that we are a very happy couple.

ROWLEY

I understand you. But then you must be very careful not to differ while he is in the house with you.

SIR PETER

Egad, and so we must—and that's impossible. Ah, Master   85 Rowley, when an old bachelor marries a young wife, he deserves—no, the crime carries its punishment along with it.

Exeunt

---

66 *fifteen years* Tickell, Murray (sixteen years   MSS). No satisfactory explanation has been suggested for this minor alteration.

75 *together* Tickell, MSS (together—hours of rough mirth, and jolly scrapes, which I dare swear he has not forgot   Spunge). An insight into the younger Sir Peter.

76 *steady to his text* true to his word

81 *Noll* diminutive of Oliver

Act II, Scene i

SIR PETER*'s house*
Enter SIR PETER *and* LADY TEAZLE

SIR PETER
Lady Teazle, Lady Teazle, I'll not bear it!

LADY TEAZLE
Sir Peter, Sir Peter, you may bear it or not as you please; but I ought to have my own way in everything—and what's more, I will too. What, though I was educated in the country, I know very well that women of fashion in London are accountable to   5
nobody after they are married.

SIR PETER
Very well, ma'am, very well. So a husband is to have no influence, no authority?

LADY TEAZLE
Authority? No, to be sure. If you wanted authority over me, you should have adopted me and not married me. I am sure   10
you were old enough.

SIR PETER
Old enough! Aye—there it is. Well, well, Lady Teazle, though my life may be made unhappy by your temper, I'll not be ruined by your extravagance.

LADY TEAZLE
My extravagance! I'm sure I am not more extravagant than a   15
woman of fashion ought to be.

SIR PETER
No, no, madam, you shall throw away no more sums on such unmeaning luxury. 'Slife, to spend as much to furnish your dressing-room with flowers in winter as would suffice to turn the Pantheon into a greenhouse and give a *fête champêtre* at   20
Christmas!

0 s.d. 1 The same set and location as the previous scene, the act curtain indicating the passage of time.

2 *Sir Peter, Sir Peter* 'Here and often in the rest of the scene Lady Teazle is mimicking her husband's repetitiveness.' (Bateson)

18 *'Slife* God's life, one of Sir Peter's many oaths and exclamations

20 *Pantheon* large public building in Oxford Street, opened 1772, modelled on the Pantheon in Rome, used for concerts and other diversions; see F. Burney, *Evelina*, Letter XXIII.
fête champêtre elegant picnic party

LADY TEAZLE

Lord, Sir Peter, am I to blame because flowers are dear in cold
weather? You should find fault with the climate and not with
me. For my part, I'm sure I wish it was spring all the year
round and that roses grew under one's feet!   25

SIR PETER

Oons, madam, if you had been born to this, I shouldn't wonder
at your talking thus. But you forget what your situation was
when I married you.

LADY TEAZLE

No, no, I don't. 'Twas a very disagreeable one, or I should
never have married you.   30

SIR PETER

Yes, yes, madam, you were then in somewhat an humbler
style—the daughter of a plain country squire. Recollect, Lady
Teazle, when I saw you first, sitting at your tambour in a pretty
figured linen gown with a bunch of keys by your side, your hair
combed smooth over a roll, and your apartment hung round   35
with fruits in worsted of your own working.

LADY TEAZLE

Oh, yes! I remember it very well, and a curious life I led—my
daily occupation to inspect the dairy, superintend the poultry,
make extracts from the family receipt-book, and comb my aunt
Deborah's lap-dog.   40

SIR PETER

Yes, yes, ma'am, 'twas so indeed.

---

26 *Oons* God's wounds; compare *Zounds*, l. 76.

31–46 Humourous descriptions of the simple life of the young lady in the country are found
frequently in eighteenth-century writers, e.g. Pope's 'An Epistle to Miss Blount, on her
leaving the Town, after the Coronation' (published 1717).

31 *an humbler* Tickell, MSS (a humbler Murray). Words of French origin with initial 'h'
were until the nineteenth century pronounced as in French with a silent 'h' and so took
the *an* form of the indefinite article.

33 *tambour* wooden frame of two concentric circles which holds a piece of cloth for
embroidering

36 *fruits in worsted* pictures of fruit embroidered in fine wool (i.e. not silk)

39 *receipt-book* recipe book

40 *Deborah* Such Old Testament Christian names, favoured by Puritans in the seven-
teenth century, were now unfashionable; compare IV.i.41 and 'in the country, where
you lived in the parsonage house ... with no other company to converse with than the
melancholy tombstones, where you read the high and mighty characters of John
Hodge and Deborah his wife.' Arthur Murphy, *Know Your Own Mind, F and M,* II,
p. 183.

LADY TEAZLE

And then, you know my evening amusements—to draw
patterns for ruffles which I had not the materials to make up;
to play Pope Joan with the curate; to read a sermon to my aunt;
or to be stuck down to an old spinet to strum my father to   45
sleep after a fox-chase.

SIR PETER

I am glad you have so good a memory. Yes, madam, these were
the recreations I took you from; but now you must have your
coach—*vis-à-vis*—and three powdered footmen before your
chair, and in the summer a pair of white cats to draw you to   50
Kensington Gardens. No recollection, I suppose, when you
were content to ride double behind the butler on a docked
coach-horse.

LADY TEAZLE

No—I swear I never did that. I deny the butler and the coach-
horse.   55

SIR PETER

This, madam, was your situation; and what have I done for
you? I have made you a woman of fashion, of fortune, of
rank—in short, I have made you my wife.

LADY TEAZLE

Well, then—and there is but one thing more you can make me
to add to the obligation, and that is—   60

---

44 *Pope Joan* game played for stakes with a pack of cards, minus the eight of diamonds,
and a board and counters
sermon Tickell, MSS, Spunge (novel   Georgetown). In a letter of 1772 Sheridan declared
that when reading 'for Entertainment' he preferred to 'view the Characters of Life as I
would wish they *were* than as they *are*: therefore I hate novels, and love Romances'.
Novels portrayed not even nature but a 'vicious and corrupt society' (*Letters*, I, 61–2).

45–6 *spinet ... sleep* Another frequent element in the image of the bored young lady in the
country; compare Sophie playing to her father, Squire Western, in Fielding's *The
History of Tom Jones*, Bk. IV, ch. v.

49 *vis à vis* carriage where the two passengers sit opposite each other
powdered footmen i.e. with powdered wigs; servants preserved this fashion after their
masters discarded wigs and wore their own hair powdered

50 *chair* i.e. sedan chair
cats Not as yet explained; the early draft has 'a pair of coach Dogs' (Redford, p. 82–3).
Both possibly mock a ladies' fashion for very small carriages and horses; compare
duodecimo phaeton II.ii.7–8, and 'A set of bays scarce bigger than six mice', Colman,
Prologue to Garrick's *Bon-Ton*, quoted in Price, p. 375.

51 *Kensington Gardens* fashionable place to walk; 'there is better company in Kensington
Gardens', *Evelina*, Letter X.

SIR PETER

My widow, I suppose?

LADY TEAZLE

Hem! Hem!

SIR PETER

Thank you, madam. But don't flatter yourself; for, though your
ill conduct may disturb my peace, it shall never break my heart,
I promise you. However, I am equally obliged to you for the   65
hint.

LADY TEAZLE

Then why will you endeavour to make yourself so disagreeable
to me and thwart me in every little elegant expense?

SIR PETER

'Slife, madam, I say—had you any of these little elegant
expenses when you married me?   70

LADY TEAZLE

Lud, Sir Peter, would you have me be out of the fashion?

SIR PETER

The fashion, indeed! What had you to do with the fashion
before you married me?

LADY TEAZLE

For my part, I should think you would like to have your wife
thought a woman of taste.   75

SIR PETER

Aye! There again! Taste! Zounds, madam, you had no taste
when you married me.

LADY TEAZLE

That's very true indeed, Sir Peter. After having married you I
should never pretend to taste again, I allow. But now, Sir Peter,
if we have finished our daily jangle, I presume I may go to my   80
engagement at Lady Sneerwell's.

SIR PETER

Aye, there's another precious circumstance. A charming set of
acquaintance you have made there!

---

79 *pretend to taste again, I allow* Tickell, Georgetown in Sheridan's hand (married you I
am sure I should never pretend to taste again   other MSS)

LADY TEAZLE

Nay, Sir Peter, they are all people of rank and fortune, and remarkably tenacious of reputation.   85

SIR PETER

Yes, egad, they are tenacious of reputation with a vengeance; for they don't choose anybody should have a character but themselves. Such a crew! Ah, many a wretch has rid on a hurdle who has done less mischief than these utterers of forged tales, coiners of scandal, and clippers of reputation.   90

LADY TEAZLE

What, would you restrain the freedom of speech?

SIR PETER

Oh, they have made you just as bad as any one of the society.

LADY TEAZLE

Why, I believe I do bear a part with a tolerable grace. But I vow I bear no malice against the people I abuse. When I say an ill-natured thing, 'tis out of pure good humour, and I take   95 it for granted they deal exactly in the same manner with me. But, Sir Peter, you know you promised to come to Lady Sneerwell's too.

SIR PETER

Well, well, I'll call in just to look after my own character.

LADY TEAZLE

Then, indeed, you make haste after me, or you'll be too late. So   100 good-bye to ye!   *Exit*

SIR PETER

So I have gained much by my intended expostulation. Yet with what a charming air she contradicts everything I say—and how pleasingly she shows her contempt for my authority. Well,

84 *rank and fortune* the two means of entry into the fashionable world; compare Sir Peter's remark, ll. 57–8. In an early letter Sheridan wrote to his friend Grenville: 'the most familiar attachment' is possible between people of different capacities, 'possess'd in a superior degree of every natural endowment as well as acquired qualification, but where the accidental advantages of Rank and Fortune are added to them—I believe it to be impossible' (*Letters*, I, 39).

88 *rid on a hurdle* dragged to execution tied to a wooden frame, a form of punishment reserved for those convicted of treason, an offence which at that time included defacing the currency

89–90 *utterers, coiners, clippers* all currency cheats: those who put false coins into circulation, the manufacturers, and those who reduce a coin's value by cutting away the edges – and use the clippings to make other coins

100 *you make* Tickell (you must make   MSS, Murray)

though I can't make her love me, there is a great satisfaction in   105
quarrelling with her. And I think she never appears to such
advantage as when she is doing everything in her power to
plague me.   *Exit*

Act II, Scene ii

At LADY SNEERWELL'S

LADY SNEERWELL, MRS CANDOUR, CRABTREE, SIR BENJAMIN
BACKBITE, *and* [JOSEPH] SURFACE

LADY SNEERWELL

Nay, positively, we will hear it.

SURFACE

Yes, yes, the epigram, by all means.

SIR BENJAMIN

Oh, plague on't, uncle! 'Tis mere nonsense.

CRABTREE

No, no, 'fore Gad, very clever for an extempore.

SIR BENJAMIN

But, ladies, you should be acquainted with the circumstance.   5
You must know that one day last week as Lady Betty Curricle
was taking the dust in Hyde Park in a sort of duodecimo
phaeton, she desired me to write some verses on her ponies,
upon which I took out my pocket-book and in one moment
produced the following: 10

       Sure never were seen two such beautiful ponies;
       Other horses are clowns, and these—macaronis.
       Nay, to give 'em this title I'm sure isn't wrong,
       Their legs are so slim and their tails are so long.

CRABTREE

There, ladies, done in the smack of a whip, and on horseback,   15
too.

---

  0 s.d. 'Pembroke table on, and tea-things ... Servant attending the company with tea;
     card table, six striped chairs before the scene' (i.e. in front of the back flat) (Scott).
6–8 *Curricle, duodecimo phaeton* types of light carriage, drawn by two horses
  7 *duodecimo* a term for a small size book, here implying a very small phaeton; compare
     II.i.50.
11–14 Material incorporated from an earlier sketch satirizing the fashionable lady; see Moore
     I, 239–40.
  12 *macaronis* late eighteenth-century term for fops, originally fops who had toured
     Europe and affected foreign tastes

SURFACE
  A very Phoebus mounted. Indeed, Sir Benjamin!

SIR BENJAMIN
  Oh, dear sir! Trifles, trifles.

Enter LADY TEAZLE *and* MARIA

MRS CANDOUR
  I must have a copy.

LADY SNEERWELL
  Lady Teazle! I hope we shall see Sir Peter?   20

LADY TEAZLE
  I believe he'll wait on your ladyship presently.

LADY SNEERWELL
  Maria, my love, you look grave. Come, you shall sit down to
  piquet with Mr Surface.

MARIA
  I take very little pleasure in cards; however, I'll do as your
  ladyship pleases.   25

LADY TEAZLE
  [*Aside*] I am surprised Mr Surface should sit down with her; I
  thought he would have embraced this opportunity of speaking
  to me before Sir Peter came.

MRS CANDOUR
  (*Coming forward*) Now, I'll die, but you are so scandalous, I'll
  forswear your society.   30

LADY TEAZLE
  What's the matter, Mrs Candour?

MRS CANDOUR
  They'll not allow our friend Miss Vermillion to be handsome.

LADY SNEERWELL
  Oh surely, she is a pretty woman.

CRABTREE
  I am very glad you think so, ma'am.

MRS CANDOUR
  She has a charming fresh colour.   35

17 *Phoebus* Phoebus Apollo, Greek god of poetry
23 *piquet* Tickell, most MSS (cards   Georgetown, Crewe B); a card game for two. Lady
    Sneerwell contrives to place Joseph and Maria together.
29 s.d. *Coming forward* Crewe B, in Sheridan's hand. She has been engaged with Sir
    Benjamin and Crabtree.

LADY TEAZLE

Yes, when it is fresh put on.

MRS CANDOUR

Oh, fie! I'll swear her colour is natural. I have seen it come and go.

LADY TEAZLE

I dare say you have, ma'am: it goes off at night and comes again in the morning.

SIR BENJAMIN

True, ma'am, it not only comes, and goes, but what's more, egad, her maid can fetch and carry it.   40

MRS CANDOUR

Ha, ha, ha! How I hate to hear you talk so. But surely now, her sister is—or *was*—very handsome.

CRABTREE

Who? Mrs Evergreen? Oh Lord, she's six and fifty if she's an hour!   45

MRS CANDOUR

Now positively you wrong her. Fifty-two or fifty-three is the utmost—and I don't think she looks more.

SIR BENJAMIN

Ah, there is no judging by her looks unless one could see her face.

LADY SNEERWELL

Well, well, if Mrs Evergreen does take some pains to repair the ravages of time, you must allow she effects it with great ingenuity; and surely that's better than the careless manner in which the Widow Ochre caulks her wrinkles.   50

SIR BENJAMIN

Nay, now Lady Sneerwell, you are severe upon the Widow. Come, come, it is not that she paints so ill—but, when she has finished her face, she joins it on so badly to her neck that she looks like a mended statue, in which the connoisseur sees at once that the head's modern, though the trunk's antique.   55

CRABTREE

Ha, ha, ha! Well said, nephew!

40   *True, ma'am,* Tickell (True Uncle   F Court, Lord C)
40–1   *it not . . . carry it.* Tickell, F Court, Lord C (not in other MSS)
   53   *Ochre* mineral earth, ranging in colour from yellow to brown, used from antiquity for painting
       caulks fills in (the cracks of her wrinkles), as in to caulk a ship, to stop up the seams

MRS CANDOUR

Ha, ha, ha! Well, you make me laugh, but I vow I hate you for 60
it. What do you think of Miss Simper?

SIR BENJAMIN

Why, she has very pretty teeth.

LADY TEAZLE

Yes; and on that account, when she is neither speaking nor
laughing (which very seldom happens), she never absolutely
shuts her mouth, but leaves it always on a jar, as it were. 65

MRS CANDOUR

How can you be so ill-natured?

LADY TEAZLE

Nay, I allow even that's better than the pains Mrs Prim takes to
conceal her losses in front. She draws her mouth till it
positively resembles the aperture of a poor's-box and all her
words appear to slide out edgeways. 70

LADY SNEERWELL

Very well, Lady Teazle; I see you can be a little severe.

LADY TEAZLE

In defence of a friend it is but justice. But here comes Sir Peter
to spoil our pleasantry.

Enter SIR PETER TEAZLE

SIR PETER

Ladies, your most obedient. (*Aside*) Mercy on me, here is the
whole set. A character dead at every word, I suppose. 75

MRS CANDOUR

I am rejoiced you are come, Sir Peter. They have been so
censorious—and Lady Teazle as bad as anyone.

65   *as it were* Tickell, MSS, 1779, Scott (as it were,—thus. (*Shows her teeth*)   Murray). Lady
Teazle's demonstration, an actor's gag, also appears in Dublin 1780 and later Dublin
editions.

70   *edgeways* Tickell, MSS, 1779, Scott (edgewise, as it were,—thus—*How do you do,
madam? Yes, madam*   Murray). The imitation of Mrs Prim also appears in the Dublin
editions.

74   s.d. *Aside* Georgetown

75   *character dead at every word* Echoing Pope's *The Rape of the Lock*, III, 16, 'At ev'ry word
a reputation dies'.

SIR PETER

It must be very distressing to *you*, Mrs Candour, I dare swear.

MRS CANDOUR

Oh, they will allow good qualities to nobody—not even good
nature to our friend Mrs Pursy.   80

LADY TEAZLE

What, the fat dowager who was at Mrs Codille's last night?

MRS CANDOUR

Nay, her bulk is her misfortune; and when she takes such pains
to get rid of it, you ought not to reflect on her.

LADY SNEERWELL

That's very true, indeed.

LADY TEAZLE

Yes, I know she almost lives on acids and small whey; laces   85
herself by pulleys; and often in the hottest noon of summer,
you may see her on a little squat pony, with her hair plaited up
behind like a drummer's, and puffing round the Ring on a full
trot.

MRS CANDOUR

I thank you, Lady Teazle, for defending her.   90

SIR PETER

Yes, a good defence truly.

MRS CANDOUR

But Sir Benjamin is as censorious as Miss Sallow.

CRABTREE

Yes, and she is a curious being to pretend to be censorious—an
awkward gawky without any one good point under Heaven!

MRS CANDOUR

Positively you shall not be so very severe. Miss Sallow is a near   95
relation of mine by marriage, and as for her person, great
allowance is to be made; for let me tell you a woman labours
under many disadvantages who tries to pass for a girl at six and
thirty.

77–9 *censorious—and Lady Teazle … Oh, they will* Tickell, F Court, Lord C (censorious—
        they will   Georgetown, Crewe B, Buck)
  80 *Pursy* Short-winded, Fat
  81 *Codille's* Codille was a term in the fashionable card game ombre.
  85 *acids* sour substances, e.g. vinegar
87–8 *hair plaited up behind* Reworked from the satirical fragment (see note at l. 11): 'Then
        behind all my hair is done up in a plait / And so, like a cornet's, tucked under my hat'.
  88 *the Ring* fashionable parade for riding and driving in Hyde Park

LADY SNEERWELL

Though surely she is handsome still—and for the weakness in   100
her eyes, considering how much she reads by candlelight it is
not to be wondered at.

MRS CANDOUR

True, and then as to her manner—upon my word I think it is
particularly graceful considering she never had the least
education. For you know her mother was a Welsh milliner and   105
her father a sugar-baker at Bristol.

SIR BENJAMIN

Ah, you are both of you too good-natured.

SIR PETER

(*Aside*) Yes, damned good-natured! This their own relation!
Mercy on me!

MRS CANDOUR

For my part I own I cannot bear to hear a friend ill spoken of.   110

SIR PETER

No, to be sure!

SIR BENJAMIN

Oh, you are of a moral turn. Mrs Candour and I can sit for an
hour and hear Lady Stucco talk sentiments.

LADY TEAZLE

Nay, I vow Lady Stucco is very well with the dessert after
dinner; for she's just like the French fruit one cracks for   115
mottoes—made up of paint and proverb.

MRS CANDOUR

Well, I never will join in ridiculing a friend—and so I
constantly tell my cousin Ogle, and you all know what
pretensions she has to be critical in beauty.

---

106 *sugar-baker* manufacturer of loaf sugar
108 s.d. *Aside* Georgetown
110–12 *For my part ... and I can* Tickell, Lord C (SIR BENJAMIN And Mrs Candour is of so moral
a turn—she can   Georgetown, not in Crewe B). In the longer Tickell version Sir
Benjamin replies possibly to Sir Peter, missing his irony, but more likely to Mrs
Candour, and then turns to Lady Teazle with *Mrs Candour and I.*
113 *Stucco* Yet another satirical allusion to heavy make up, and recalling, in the image of
the plastered wall, Lady Wishfort in Congreve's *The Way of the World*: 'I look like an
old peel'd wall' (III.i).
sentiments Tickell, F Court, Lord C (sentiment   Georgetown)
115–16 *French fruit ... proverb* hollow sugar confections containing mottoes; compare fortune
cookies.

CRABTREE

O, to be sure. She has herself the oddest countenance that ever   120
was seen. 'Tis a collection of features from all the different
countries of the globe.

SIR BENJAMIN

So she has indeed. An Irish front ...

CRABTREE

Caledonian locks ...

SIR BENJAMIN

Dutch nose ...   125

CRABTREE

Austrian lip ...

SIR BENJAMIN

Complexion of a Spaniard ...

CRABTREE

And teeth *à la Chinoise*!

SIR BENJAMIN

In short, her face resembles a *table d'hôte* at Spa, where no two
guests are of a nation—

                                                        130

CRABTREE

Or a congress at the close of a general war—wherein all the
members, even to her eyes, appear to have a different interest,
and her nose and chin are the only parties likely to join issue.

MRS CANDOUR

Ha, ha, ha!

SIR PETER

(*Aside*) Mercy on my life—a person they dine with twice a   135
week.

LADY SNEERWELL

Go, go; you are a couple of provoking toads.

---

123 *Irish* No characteristic suggests itself; this and the following insults may not have much
     point apart from their xenophobia.
     front forehead
124 *Caledonian locks* long hair, like a Highland Scot's
125 *Dutch nose* 'Flat or snub-nosed' (Bateson)
126 *Austrian lip* protruding lower lip, an inherited jaw deformity in the Hapsburg dynasty
127 *Complexion of a Spaniard* Dark-skinned
128 *teeth à la Chinoise* black, an effect of eating opium
129 *table d'hôte* the common dining-table in an inn
     Spa Belgian town renowned for its mineral springs
135 s.d. *Aside* Georgetown
137 *Go ... toads* Tickell, F Court, Lord C (not in Georgetown, Crewe B, Buck)

MRS CANDOUR

Nay, but I vow you shall not carry the laugh off so. For give me
leave to say that Mrs Ogle—

SIR PETER

Madam, madam, I beg your pardon. There's no stopping these   140
good gentlemen's tongues. But when I tell you, Mrs Candour,
that the lady they are abusing is a particular friend of mine, I
hope you'll not take her part.

LADY SNEERWELL

Ha, ha, ha! Well said, Sir Peter! But you are a cruel creature,
too phlegmatic yourself for a jest, and too peevish to allow wit   145
in others.

SIR PETER

Ah, madam, true wit is more nearly allied to good nature than
your ladyship is aware of.

LADY TEAZLE

True, Sir Peter, I believe they are so near akin that they can
never be united.   150

SIR BENJAMIN

Or rather, madam, suppose them to be man and wife, because
one seldom sees them together.

LADY TEAZLE

But Sir Peter is such an enemy to scandal I believe he would
have it put down by Parliament.

SIR PETER

'Fore Heaven, madam, if they were to consider the sporting   155
with reputation of as much importance as poaching on manors
and pass an Act for the Preservation of Fame, I believe there are
many would thank them for the Bill.

LADY SNEERWELL

O lud, Sir Peter, would you deprive us of our privileges?

SIR PETER

Aye, madam; and then no person should be permitted to kill   160

---

147   *wit ... good nature* Sir Peter continues from I.ii. the debate about the nature of 'true
        wit'.
149–50 *so near ... united* Alluding to those who are closely related being 'forbidden in scrip-
        ture and our laws' (in the Book of Common Prayer) from marrying.
156   *manors* in the legal sense of the land owned by Lords of the Manor
157   *Preservation of Fame* The unspoken rhyme with 'game' points Sir Peter's witty attack
        on 'sporting with reputation'.

characters or run down reputations, but qualified old maids and disappointed widows.

LADY SNEERWELL

Go, you monster!

MRS CANDOUR

But sure you would not be quite so severe on those who only report what they hear?   165

SIR PETER

Yes, madam, I would have law merchant for them too; and in all cases of slander currency, whenever the drawer of the lie was not to be found, the injured parties should have a right to come on any of the endorsers.

CRABTREE

Well, for my part I believe there never was a scandalous tale   170
without some foundation.

SIR PETER

Oh, nine out of ten of the malicious inventions are founded on some ridiculous misrepresentation.

LADY SNEERWELL

Come, ladies, shall we sit down to cards in the next room?

Enter SERVANT, *and whispers* SIR PETER

SIR PETER

I'll be with them directly.   175

[*Exit* SERVANT]

[*Aside*] I'll get away unperceived.

LADY TEAZLE

Sir Peter, you are not going to leave us?

---

166   *law merchant* i.e. law regulating merchants; Sir Peter follows *sporting* with reputations with wordplay on *trading* in gossip.

167   *of slander currency* of circulating slander

167–9   *drawer ... endorsers* Continuing the parallels between money and gossip: here the *drawer* who writes a cheque and the *endorsers* who put their signature to it are likened to the one who puts a lie around and those who vouch for its truth.
  endorsers literally, those responsible if the drawer fails to pay

172–3   *Oh, nine ... misrepresentation* Tickell, Murray, Lord C (not in Georgetown, not noticed in Price). The remark recalls the fanciful stories circulating in Bath after Sheridan's second duel and his remark: 'Let me see what they report of me today; I wish to know whether I am dead or alive.' (Alicia Lefanu, *Memoirs of ... Frances Sheridan* (1824), p. 406, qtd. in Kelly, p. 47.)

SIR PETER

Your ladyship must excuse me; I'm called away by particular
business. But I leave my character behind me.   *Exit*

SIR BENJAMIN

Well, certainly, Lady Teazle, that lord of yours is a strange   180
being. I could tell you some stories of him would make you
laugh heartily if he were not your husband.

LADY TEAZLE

Oh, pray don't mind that. Come, do let's hear them.

Joins the rest of the company going into the next room

SURFACE

(*Rising with* MARIA) Maria, I see you have no satisfaction in this
society.   185

MARIA

How is it possible I should? If to raise malicious smiles at the
infirmities or misfortunes of those who have never injured us
be the province of wit or humour, Heaven grant me a double
portion of dullness!

SURFACE

Yet they appear more ill-natured than they are. They have no   190
malice at heart.

MARIA

Then is their conduct still more contemptible, for, in my
opinion, nothing could excuse the intemperance of their
tongues but a natural and ungovernable bitterness of mind.

SURFACE

Undoubtedly, madam; and it has always been a sentiment of   195
mine that to propagate a malicious truth wantonly is more
despicable than to falsify from revenge. But can you, Maria, feel
thus for others and be unkind to me alone? Is hope to be
denied the tenderest passion?

MARIA

Why will you distress me by renewing the subject?   200

183 s.d. *Joins . . . room* Tickell (*Joins the rest of the company, all talking as they are going into
the next room*   Georgetown, Crewe B; *Join the rest of the company all talking and going
into the next room M*[iddle] *D*[oor]   Scott). All versions indicate a long exit by a door
in the back flat.
184 s.d. *Rising with* MARIA Georgetown, in Sheridan's hand
193 *intemperance* F Court, Georgetown, Spunge, Bateson (interference   Lord C, Tickell,
Murray). Tickell perpetuates the early Lord C misreading.
195–7 *Undoubtedly . . . from revenge* Tickell, Murray, F Court, Lord C (not in other MSS)

SURFACE

Ah, Maria, you would not treat me thus and oppose your guardian Sir Peter's will, but that I see that profligate Charles is still a favoured rival.

MARIA

Ungenerously urged! But whatever my sentiments are for that unfortunate young man, be assured I shall not feel more bound   205
to give him up because his distresses have lost him the regard even of a brother.

[*Enter* LADY TEAZLE]

SURFACE

Nay, but Maria, do not leave me with a frown. [*Kneels*] By all that's honest I swear— (*Aside*) Gad's life, here's Lady Teazle. –
You must not—no, you shall not—for though I have the   210
greatest regard for Lady Teazle—

MARIA

Lady Teazle!

[SURFACE *rises*]

SURFACE

Yet, were Sir Peter to suspect—

[LADY TEAZLE] *comes forward*

LADY TEAZLE

What is this pray, do you take her for me?—Child, you are wanted in the next room.   215

Exit MARIA

What is all this, pray?

204–5 *are for that unfortunate young man* Tickell, Murray (of that unfortunate young man are MSS)

207 s.d. *[Enter* LADY TEAZLE*]* ed. (LADY TEAZLE *returns* Georgetown; *Enter* LADY TEAZLE *and comes forward* Tickell, after 'suspect', l. 213). This is a long entry, the audience seeing Lady Teazle before Joseph does.

208 *do not leave me* Dublin 1780 has s.d. *Going out* after 'brother', l. 207, to mark Maria's attempt to leave.

208 s.d. *Kneels* ed. No indications survive in authoritative texts of when Joseph should kneel or get up. Here, Joseph kneels, then sees Lady Teazle, as in Dublin 1780: *Kneels and sees Lady Teazle entering behind*, and delays rising, framing his speech to deceive her.

209 s.d. *Aside* Georgetown

213 s.d. *comes forward* Crewe B (*coming forward* Georgetown)

SURFACE

Oh, the most unlucky circumstance in nature. Maria has somehow suspected the tender concern which I have for your happiness and threatened to acquaint Sir Peter with her suspicions, and I was just endeavouring to reason with her   220
when you came in.

LADY TEAZLE

Indeed! But you seem to adopt a very tender mode of reasoning. Do you usually argue on your knees?

SURFACE

Oh, she's a child and I thought a little bombast—but, Lady Teazle, when are you to give me your judgment on my library,   225
as you promised?

LADY TEAZLE

No, no; I begin to think it would be imprudent, and you know I admit you as a lover no farther than fashion requires.

SURFACE

True—a mere Platonic *cicisbeo*—what every wife is entitled to.

LADY TEAZLE

Certainly one must not be out of the fashion. However, I have   230
so much of my country prejudices left that, though Sir Peter's ill humour may vex me ever so, it shall never provoke me to—

SURFACE

The only revenge in your power. Well, I applaud your moderation.

LADY TEAZLE

Go! You are an insinuating wretch! But we shall be missed. Let   235
us join the company.

SURFACE

But we had best not return together.

222   *mode* Tickell (method   MSS)
224   *bombast* inflated speech, accompanied here with the grand gesture – the lover kneeling
      at the lady's feet
225   *my library* Compare the innuendo associated with the rake Horner's 'china' in *The
      Country Wife*.
228   *requires* Tickell, MSS (sanctions   Murray)
229   *Platonic cicisbeo* married woman's recognized gallant, *cavalier servente*, but not a lover;
      his privileges (few) and duties (light) are detailed in Frances Sheridan, *A Journey to
      Bath*, III.i, p.185.
      wife Tickell, Lord C, Crewe B (London wife   F Court, Georgetown). The omission of
      London suits Joseph: *wife* means London wife, no other is of interest to him.
231   *country prejudices* i.e. a sense of morality: is Lady Teazle's phrase consciously ironic?

LADY TEAZLE

Well, don't stay, for Maria shan't come to hear any more of your reasoning, I promise you.   *Exit*

SURFACE

A curious dilemma my politics have run me into! I wanted at   240
first only to ingratiate myself with Lady Teazle that she might
not be my enemy with Maria; and I have, I don't know how,
become her serious lover. Sincerely I begin to wish I had never
made such a point of gaining so very good a character, for it
has led me into so many cursed rogueries that I doubt I shall be   245
exposed at last.   *Exit*

Act II, Scene iii

SIR PETER TEAZLE's
Enter SIR OLIVER SURFACE *and* ROWLEY

SIR OLIVER

Ha, ha, ha! So my old friend is married, hey? A young wife out
of the country. Ha, ha, ha! That he should have stood bluff to
old bachelor so long and sink into a husband at last.

ROWLEY

But you must not rally him on the subject, Sir Oliver. 'Tis a
tender point, I assure you, though he has been married only   5
seven months.

SIR OLIVER

Then he has been just half a year on the stool of repentance!
Poor Peter! But you say he has entirely given up Charles—
never sees him, hey?

ROWLEY

His prejudice against him is astonishing, and I am sure greatly   10
increased by a jealousy of him with Lady Teazle, which he has
been industriously led into by a scandalous society in the
neighbourhood, who have contributed not a little to Charles's
ill name; whereas the truth is, I believe, if the lady is partial to
either of them, his brother is the favourite.   15

240 *politics* scheming, cunning
  0 s.d. The Scott promptbook specifies this is an 'Antique Chamber'.
  2 *stood bluff* stuck boldly to his status, i.e. as old bachelor
  4 *rally* make fun of, a late seventeenth-century word. Compare 'raillery', and see note at
     I.i.87.
  7 *stool of repentance* low stool where offenders sat during the service in Scottish churches

SIR OLIVER

Aye, I know there are a set of malicious, prating, prudent gossips, both male and female, who murder characters to kill time, and will rob a young fellow of his good name before he has years to know the value of it. But I am not to be prejudiced against my nephew by such, I promise you. No, no, if Charles has done nothing false or mean, I shall compound for his extravagance.   20

ROWLEY

Then, my life on't, you will reclaim him. Ah, sir, it gives me new life to find that *your* heart is not turned against him, and that the son of my good old master has one friend however left.   25

SIR OLIVER

What, shall I forget, Master Rowley, when I was at his years myself? Egad, my brother and I were neither of us very prudent youths—and yet, I believe, you have not seen many better men than your old master was.

ROWLEY

Sir, 'tis this reflection gives me assurance that Charles may yet be a credit to his family. But here comes Sir Peter.   30

SIR OLIVER

Egad, so he does! Mercy on me, he's greatly altered, and seems to have a settled married look. One may read husband in his face at this distance!

Enter SIR PETER [TEAZLE]

SIR PETER

Hah! Sir Oliver—my old friend. Welcome to England a thousand times!   35

SIR OLIVER

Thank you—thank you, Sir Peter! And i'faith I am as glad to find you well, believe me.

SIR PETER

Oh, 'tis a long time since we met—fifteen years, I doubt, Sir Oliver, and many a cross accident in the time.   40

---

16 *prating,* idly chattering
   prudent worldly wise ('practically wise', Johnson's *Dictionary*); compare Sir Oliver's remark on prudence, ll. 75–7; for a less critical sense, see l. 27.

21 *compound* settle up, pay

39 *fifteen years* See note at I.ii.66.

SIR OLIVER

Aye, I have had my share. But what—I find you are married, hey?
Well, well, it can't be helped, and so I wish you joy with all my heart.

SIR PETER

Thank you, thank you, Sir Oliver. Yes, I have entered into the
happy state. But we'll not talk of that now.

SIR OLIVER

True, true, Sir Peter. Old friends should not begin on   45
grievances at first meeting. No, no, no.

ROWLEY

(*To* SIR OLIVER) Take care, pray, sir.

SIR OLIVER

Well—so one of my nephews is a wild rogue, hey?

SIR PETER

Wild! Ah, my old friend, I grieve for your disappointment
there; he's a lost young man, indeed. However, his brother will   50
make you amends; Joseph is, indeed, what a youth should be.
Everybody in the world speaks well of him.

SIR OLIVER

I am sorry to hear it; he has too good a character to be an
honest fellow. Everybody speaks well of him! Pshaw! Then he
has bowed as low to knaves and fools as to the honest dignity   55
of genius and virtue.

SIR PETER

What, Sir Oliver, do you blame him for not making enemies?

SIR OLIVER

Yes, if he has merit enough to deserve them.

SIR PETER

Well, well—you'll be convinced when you know him. 'Tis
edification to hear him converse; he professes the noblest   60
sentiments.

SIR OLIVER

Oh, plague of his sentiments! If he salutes me with a scrap of
morality in his mouth, I shall be sick directly. But, however,
don't mistake me, Sir Peter; I don't mean to defend Charles's

41 *hey?* Tickell (hey, my old boy?   MSS)
47 *To* SIR OLIVER Georgetown, in Sheridan's hand
53 *character* reputation; compare II.ii.161, but elsewhere in the play used to mean person-
    ality, nature.
60 *edification* instruction leading to moral, spiritual improvement, a word with Puritan
    associations

[82]

errors. But before I form my judgment of either of them, I   65
intend to make a trial of their hearts; and my friend Rowley
and I have planned something for the purpose.

ROWLEY

And Sir Peter shall own, for once, he has been mistaken.

SIR PETER

Oh, my life on Joseph's honour!

SIR OLIVER

Well, come, give us a bottle of good wine, and we'll drink the   70
lads' health, and tell you our scheme.

SIR PETER

Allons, then!

SIR OLIVER

And don't, Sir Peter, be so severe against your old friend's son.
Odds my life! I am not sorry that he has run out of the course a
little. For my part I hate to see prudence clinging to the green   75
suckers of youth; 'tis like ivy round a sapling and spoils the
growth of the tree.

Exeunt

Act III, Scene i

SIR PETER TEAZLE'*s*
Enter SIR PETER [TEAZLE], SIR OLIVER [SURFACE] *and* ROWLEY
[*and* SERVANT]

SIR PETER

Well then, we will see this fellow first and have our wine
afterwards. But how is this, Master Rowley? I don't see the jet
of your scheme.

ROWLEY

Why, sir, this Mr Stanley who I was speaking of is nearly related
to them by their mother. He was once a merchant in Dublin   5
but has been ruined by a series of undeserved misfortunes. He

---

68   *for once, he has been* Tickell (he has been for once   MSS)
74   *Odds my life!* God's my life!
 0   s.d. i.e. the same location as the previous scene, with the Act curtain indicating the
     passage of time (as between Acts I and II)
 2   *jet* point

has applied by letter to Mr Surface and Charles. From the former he has received nothing but evasive promises of future service, while Charles has done all that his extravagance has left him power to do; and he is at this time endeavouring to raise a sum of money, part of which, in the midst of his own distresses, I know he intends for the service of poor Stanley. 10

SIR OLIVER

Ah, he is my brother's son.

SIR PETER

Well, but how is Sir Oliver personally to—

ROWLEY

Why, sir, I will inform Charles and his brother that Stanley has 15 obtained permission to apply personally to his friends; and, as they have neither of them ever seen him, let Sir Oliver assume his character and he will have a fair opportunity of judging at least of the benevolence of their dispositions. And believe me, sir, you will find in the youngest brother one who, in the midst of 20 folly and dissipation, has still, as our immortal bard expresses it,

a tear for pity and a hand,
Open as the day for melting charity.

SIR PETER

Pshaw! What signifies his having an open hand, or purse either, when he has nothing left to give? Well, well, make the trial if 25 you please. But where is the fellow whom you brought for Sir Oliver to examine relative to Charles's affairs?

ROWLEY

Below, waiting his commands, and no one can give him better intelligence. This, Sir Oliver, is a friendly Jew, who to do him justice has done everything in his power to bring your nephew 30 to a proper sense of his extravagance.

---

7   *by letter* Tickell, F Court (by letter since his confinement   MSS). Perhaps a polite dele-
tion? In 1814 and 1815 (after the date of the Tickell MS) Sheridan himself was arrested
and held for debt.

11   *distresses* financial embarrassments, specifically, the seizing of a debtor's goods; compare ll. 94, 150, and I.i.99.

16   *apply personally* Tickell, Murray (apply in person   MSS). That is, to leave his confinement and apply to his friends for help.

20   *youngest* Tickell, MSS (younger   Murray). Compare other Murray corrections at I.ii.3
and III.i.257.

22–3   *a tear ... charity* Tickell (a heart to pity ... charity   Murray). This is quoting *2 Henry
IV*, IV.iv. 31–2 (from the dying King Henry's speech on Prince Hal), adding 'the' after
'as', as do some MSS.

SIR PETER

Pray, let us have him in.

ROWLEY

[*To* SERVANT] Desire Mr Moses to walk upstairs.

[*Exit* SERVANT]

SIR PETER

But, pray, why should you suppose that he will speak the
truth?   35

ROWLEY

Oh, I have convinced him that he has no chance of recovering
certain sums advanced to Charles but through the bounty of Sir
Oliver, who he knows is arrived, so that you may depend on his
fidelity to his own interest. I have also another evidence in my
power, one Snake, whom I have detected in a matter little short   40
of forgery, and shall shortly produce to remove some of your
prejudices.

SIR PETER

I have heard too much on that subject.

ROWLEY

Here comes the honest Israelite.

Enter MOSES

This is Sir Oliver.   45

SIR OLIVER

Sir, I understand you have lately had great dealings with my
nephew Charles.

---

39 *evidence* witness
41 *shortly* Tickell, MSS (speedily   Murray)
42 *prejudices* Tickell, Murray (prejudices, Sir Peter, in relation to Charles and Lady Teazle
    Lord C, Georgetown, 1779 and others). A valuable revision, keeping the focus on
    Charles's extravagance by postponing reference to the possibility of an affair between
    Charles and Lady Teazle to l. 131, and then having Sir Peter rather than Rowley men-
    tion it first.
44 *honest Israelite* On 7 May the play was refused a license because a candidate for re-elec-
    tion as City Chamberlain, Benjamin Hopkins, (a Christian who reputedly lent money
    at high interest to minors) complained that the figure of Moses was part of a campaign
    to smear him. Since his fellow candidate was the radical Whig, John Wilkes, and
    Sheridan was already associated with the radical Whig group, he had some grounds to
    be suspicious. However, Sheridan managed to persuade the Lord Chamberlain that the
    charge had no foundation, and the first performance went ahead as planned the next
    day.

MOSES

Yes, Sir Oliver, I have done all I could for him; but he was ruined before he came to me for assistance.

SIR OLIVER

That was unlucky, truly, for you have had no opportunity of 50 showing your talents.

MOSES

None at all. I hadn't the pleasure of knowing his distresses till he was some thousands worse than nothing.

SIR OLIVER

Unfortunate, indeed! But I suppose you have done all in your power for him, honest Moses? 55

MOSES

Yes, he knows that. This very evening I was to have brought him a gentleman from the City, who does not know him and will, I believe, advance him some money.

SIR PETER

What—one Charles has never had money from before?

MOSES

Yes. Mr Premium of Crutched Friars, formerly a broker. 60

SIR PETER

Egad, Sir Oliver, a thought strikes me. Charles, you say, does not know Mr Premium?

MOSES

Not at all.

SIR PETER

Now then, Sir Oliver, you may have a better opportunity of satisfying yourself than by an old romancing tale of a poor 65 relation. Go with my friend Moses and represent Mr Premium, and then, I'll answer for it, you'll see your nephew in all his glory.

SIR OLIVER

Egad, I like this idea better than the other, and I may visit Joseph afterwards as old Stanley.

SIR PETER

True. So you may. 70

---

60 *Crutched Friars* street off Aldgate in the City where the Monastery of the Friars of the Holy Cross once stood
65 *romancing* 'fantastic, incredible (like a mediaeval romance)' (Bateson)

ROWLEY

Well, this is taking Charles rather at a disadvantage, to be sure.
However, Moses, you understand Sir Peter, and will be faithful?

MOSES

You may depend on me. This is near the time I was to have gone.

SIR OLIVER

I'll accompany you as soon as you please, Moses. But hold, I have
forgot one thing. How the plague shall I be able to pass for a Jew?   75

MOSES

There's no need. The principal is Christian.

SIR OLIVER

Is he? I'm very sorry to hear it. But then again, a'n't I rather too
smartly dressed to look like a money-lender?

SIR PETER

Not at all; 'twould not be out of character, if you went in your
own carriage. Would it, Moses?   80

MOSES

Not in the least.

SIR OLIVER

Well, but how must I talk? There's certainly some cant of usury
and mode of treating that I ought to know.

SIR PETER

Oh, there's not much to learn. The great point, as I take it, is to
be exorbitant enough in your demands—hey, Moses?   85

MOSES

Yes, that's a very great point.

SIR OLIVER

I'll answer for't I'll not be wanting in that. I'll ask him eight or
ten per cent on the loan—at least.

MOSES

If you ask him no more than that, you'll be discovered
immediately.   90

SIR OLIVER

Hey, what the plague! How much then?

MOSES

That depends upon the circumstances. If he appears not very

---

73 *depend on me* Scott has s.d. here: *Looking at his watch*
76 *The principal* in the legal sense of the chief person concerned in some proceeding, here
the man who is to lend the money
82 *cant* jargon
83 *treating* negotiating

anxious for the supply, you should require only forty or fifty
per cent. But if you find him in great distress and want the
moneys very bad, you may ask double. 95

SIR PETER

A good honest trade you're learning, Sir Oliver.

SIR OLIVER

Truly, I think so—and not unprofitable.

MOSES

Then, you know, you haven't the moneys yourself, but are
forced to borrow them for him of an old friend.

SIR OLIVER

Oh, I borrow it of a friend, do I? 100

MOSES

And your friend is an unconscionable dog; but you can't help
it.

SIR OLIVER

My friend an unconscionable dog!

MOSES

Yes, and he himself has not the money by him, but is forced to
sell stock at a great loss. 105

SIR OLIVER

He is forced to sell stock at a great loss, is he? Well, that's very
kind of him.

SIR PETER

I'faith, Sir Oliver—Mr Premium, I mean—you'll soon be
master of the trade. But Moses, wouldn't you have him run out

---

94-5 *want the moneys* Tickell, Georgetown, Crewe B, Buck (money F Court Lord C). If
there is a hint of foreign idiom here and at l. 98 (with an echo of Shylock's 'monies',
Merchant of Venice, I.iii), it is not in the pre-performance MSS. However, Baddeley
played Moses 'as a real Jew' according to a review (qtd. in Price, p. 310) and pirated
editions have 'dat' for 'that' and 'he wants money very bad' (Bateson p. xxvi). This is
the style of other stage Jews, Nathan and Moses, for instance, in Samuel Foote's *The
Nabob* (performed 1772): 'As to dat matter, I vas not inquire dat.' *F and M*, II.ii, p. 99.
103 *My friend* Tickell, Murray (My friend is MSS)
104 *the money* F Court, Lord C, Tickell (the monies other MSS, 1779, Bateson)
109 *wouldn't you* MSS, 1779, Bateson (would you Tickell). A copyist's error?
run out 'speak out boldly and profusely, expatiate' (*OED*)

a little against the Annuity Bill? That would be in character, I   110
should think.

MOSES

Very much.

ROWLEY

And lament that a young man now must be at years of
discretion before he is suffered to ruin himself?

MOSES

Aye, great pity!   115

SIR PETER

And abuse the public for allowing merit to an Act whose only
object is to snatch misfortune and imprudence from the rapacious
relief of usury—and give the minor a chance of inheriting his
estate without being undone by coming into possession.

SIR OLIVER

So—so. Moses shall give me further instructions as we go   120
together.

SIR PETER

You will not have much time, for your nephew lives hard by.

SIR OLIVER

Oh, never fear: my tutor appears so able, that though Charles
lived in the next street, it must be my own fault if I am not a
complete rogue before I turn the corner.   125

Exeunt SIR OLIVER SURFACE *and* MOSES

SIR PETER

So now I think Sir Oliver will be convinced. You are partial,
Rowley, and would have prepared Charles for the other plot.

ROWLEY

No, upon my word, Sir Peter.

SIR PETER

Well, go bring me this Snake, and I'll hear what he has to say
presently. I see Maria and want to speak with her.   130

[*Exit* ROWLEY]

110 *the Annuity Bill* Under its provisions, the Bill (passed May 1777) required annuities to
      be registered, limited the amount money lenders could ask in annual interest to 10
      shillings per £100, and made void contracts for annuities with minors (i.e. under
      twenty-one).
129 *Snake* The questioning of Snake in F Court was at first in this scene but later moved to
      V.iii.
130 *presently* at once

I should be glad to be convinced my suspicions of Lady Teazle and Charles were unjust. I have never yet opened my mind on this subject to my friend Joseph. I am determined I will do it; he will give me his opinion sincerely.

Enter MARIA

So, child, has Mr Surface returned with you?   135

MARIA

No, sir. He was engaged.

SIR PETER

Well, Maria, do you not reflect the more you converse with that amiable young man, what return his partiality for you deserves?

MARIA

Indeed, Sir Peter, your frequent importunity on this subject distresses me extremely. You compel me to declare that I know   140
no man who has ever paid me a particular attention whom I would not prefer to Mr Surface.

SIR PETER

So—here's perverseness! No, no, Maria, 'tis Charles only whom you would prefer. 'Tis evident his vices and follies have won your heart.   145

MARIA

This is unkind, sir. You know I have obeyed you in neither seeing nor corresponding with him. I have heard enough to convince me that he is unworthy my regard. Yet I cannot think it culpable, if, while my understanding severely condemns his vices, my heart suggests some pity for his distresses.   150

SIR PETER

Well, well, pity him as much as you please, but give your heart and hand to a worthier object.

MARIA

Never to his brother.

SIR PETER

Go, perverse and obstinate! But take care, madam; you have never yet known what the authority of a guardian is. Don't   155
compel me to inform you of it.

MARIA

I can only say you shall not have just reason. 'Tis true, by my father's will I am for a short period bound to regard you as his

---

135   *returned* i.e. from Lady Sneerwell's
154   *madam* Now angry, Sir Peter addresses the resistant Maria formally as an adult.

substitute, but must cease to think you so when you would
compel me to be miserable.   *Exit*   160

SIR PETER

Was ever man so crossed as I am?—everything conspiring to
fret me! I had not been involved in matrimony a fortnight
before her father, a hale and hearty man, died, on purpose I
believe, for the pleasure of plaguing me with the care of his
daughter. But here comes my helpmate. She appears in great   165
good humour. How happy I should be if I could tease her into
loving me, though but a little.

Enter LADY TEAZLE

LADY TEAZLE

Lud, Sir Peter, I hope you haven't been quarrelling with Maria?
It is not using me well to be ill-humoured when I am not by.

SIR PETER

Ah, Lady Teazle, you might have the power to make me good-   170
humoured at all times.

LADY TEAZLE

I am sure I wish I had, for I want you to be in charming sweet
temper at this moment. Do be good-humoured now and let me
have two hundred pounds, will you?

SIR PETER

Two hundred pounds! What, a'n't I to be in a good humour   175
without paying for it? But speak to me thus and i'faith there's
nothing I could refuse you. You shall have it, but seal me a
bond for the repayment.

LADY TEAZLE

Oh, no. There—my note of hand will do as well.

SIR PETER

(*Kissing her hand*) And you shall no longer reproach me with   180
not giving you an independent settlement. I mean shortly to
surprise you. But shall we always live thus, hey?

LADY TEAZLE

If you please. I'm sure I don't care how soon we leave off
quarrelling provided you'll own you were tired first.

160   s.d. *Exit* Tickell, MSS (*Exit in tears*   Dublin 1780)
165   *helpmate* Ironic, and recalling the creation of Eve to be 'an help meet' for Adam
        (Genesis 2. 18).
180   s.d. *Kissing her hand* Georgetown, in Sheridan's hand (not in Tickell; *Offering her hand*
        Murray). Sir Peter begs a kiss at *seal me a bond*; Lady Teazle offers only her hand: *my
        note of hand will do as well.*

SIR PETER

Well, then let our future contest be who shall be most obliging.   185

LADY TEAZLE

I assure you, Sir Peter, good nature becomes you. You look now as you did before we were married, when you used to walk with me under the elms and tell me stories of what a gallant you were in your youth and chuck me under the chin, you would, and ask me if I thought I could love an old fellow who   190 would deny me nothing—didn't you?

SIR PETER

Yes, yes, and you were as kind and attentive—

LADY TEAZLE

Aye, so I was, and would always take your part when my acquaintance used to abuse you and turn you into ridicule.

SIR PETER

Indeed!   195

LADY TEAZLE

Aye, and when my cousin Sophy has called you a stiff, peevish old bachelor and laughed at me for thinking of marrying one who might be my father, I have always defended you and said I didn't think you so ugly by any means—and I dared say you'd make a very good sort of a husband.   200

SIR PETER

And you prophesied right. And we shall now be the happiest couple—

LADY TEAZLE

And never differ again?

SIR PETER

No, never, though at the same time indeed, my dear Lady Teazle, you must watch your temper very seriously, for—in all   205 our little quarrels, my dear, if you recollect, my love, you always began first.

LADY TEAZLE

I beg your pardon, my dear Sir Peter. Indeed, you always gave the provocation.

SIR PETER

Now see, my angel! Take care. Contradicting isn't the way to   210 keep friends.

205 *seriously* Tickell, Murray (narrowly   MSS)
205–7 Sir Peter's short phrases convey his attempt to be diplomatic.

LADY TEAZLE

Then don't you begin it, my love.

SIR PETER

There, now, you—you are going on. You don't perceive, my
life, that you are just doing the very thing which you know
always makes me angry.   215

LADY TEAZLE

Nay, you know if you will be angry without any reason, my
dear—

SIR PETER

There, now you want to quarrel again.

LADY TEAZLE

No, I am sure I don't; but if you will be so peevish—

SIR PETER

There now! Who begins first?   220

LADY TEAZLE

Why, you to be sure. I said nothing; but there's no bearing
your temper.

SIR PETER

No, no, madam! The fault's in your own temper.

LADY TEAZLE

Aye, you are just what my cousin Sophy said you would be.

SIR PETER

Your cousin Sophy is a forward impertinent gipsy.   225

LADY TEAZLE

You are a great bear, I'm sure, to abuse my relations.

SIR PETER

Now may all the plagues of marriage be doubled on me if ever I
try to be friends with you any more!

LADY TEAZLE

So much the better.

SIR PETER

No, no, madam. 'Tis evident you never cared a pin for me   230
and I was a madman to marry you—a pert rural coquette

224–6 An anecdote survives of Sheridan rehearsing this passage with Mrs Abington: 'No, no
that won't do at all. It mustn't be *pettish*. That's shallow—shallow. You must go up
stage with, "You are just what my cousin Sophy said you would be," and then turn and
sweep down on him like a volcano. "You are a great bear to abuse my relations! How
dare you abuse my relations!"' (Price, p. 393)

225 *gipsy* here, a general term of contempt for a woman

that had refused half the honest squires in the neighbourhood.

LADY TEAZLE

And I am sure I was a fool to marry you—an old dangling bachelor, who was single at fifty only because he never could   235
meet with anyone who would have him.

SIR PETER

Aye, aye, madam; but you were pleased enough to listen to me. You never had such an offer before.

LADY TEAZLE

No? Didn't I refuse Sir Tivy Terrier, who everybody said would have been a better match, for his estate is just as good as yours   240
and he has broke his neck since we have married?

SIR PETER

I have done with you, madam. You are an unfeeling, ungrateful—but there's an end of everything. I believe you capable of anything that is bad. Yes, madam, I now believe the reports relative to you and Charles, madam. Yes, madam, you   245
and Charles are, not without grounds—

LADY TEAZLE

Take care, Sir Peter! You had better not insinuate any such thing. I'll not be suspected without cause, I promise you.

SIR PETER

Very well, madam, very well! A separate maintenance as soon as you please. Yes, madam, or a divorce! I'll make an example of   250
myself, for the benefit of all old bachelors. Let us separate, madam.

LADY TEAZLE

Agreed, agreed! And now, my dear Sir Peter, we are of a mind once more, we may be the happiest couple and never differ again, you know. Ha, ha, ha! Well, you are going to be in a passion, I see, and I shall only interrupt you; so bye, bye!   *Exit*   255

SIR PETER

Plagues and tortures! Can't I make her angry either? Oh, I am the miserablest fellow! But I'll not bear her presuming to keep her temper. No. She may break my heart, but she shan't keep her temper.   *Exit*

---

234 *dangling* hanging on, or about, 'as a loosely attached follower' (*OED*); Dangle is an
     enthusiastic theatre 'hanger on' in *The Critic*.
239 *Tivy Terrier* a name for a hunting squire; 'tantivy' is a rapid gallop.
257 *miserablest* Tickell, MSS (most miserable   Murray). Murray corrects Sir Peter's dis-
     tinctive superlative, as at I.ii.3.

Act III, Scene ii

CHARLES's *house*
Enter TRIP, MOSES, *and* SIR OLIVER [SURFACE]

TRIP

Here, Master Moses! If you'll stay a moment, I'll try whether—
what's the gentleman's name?

SIR OLIVER

(*Aside*) Mr Moses, what is my name?

MOSES

Mr Premium.

TRIP

Premium. Very well.   *Exit, taking snuff*   5

SIR OLIVER

To judge by the servants one wouldn't believe the master was
ruined. But what—sure, this was my brother's house?

MOSES

Yes, sir; Mr Charles bought it of Mr Joseph, with the furniture,
pictures, etc., just as the old gentleman left it. Sir Peter thought
it a great piece of extravagance in him.   10

SIR OLIVER

In my mind the other's economy in selling it to him was more
reprehensible by half.

Enter TRIP

TRIP

My Master says you must wait, gentlemen; he has company and
can't speak with you yet.

SIR OLIVER

If he knew who it was wanted to see him, perhaps he would not   15
send such a message.

---

 0 s.d. 'Drop Chamber' (Scott) i.e. a back cloth of a room in Charles's house let down on
     a roller
 1 *whether*— Tickell, MSS (whether Mr.—   F Court)
 3 s.d. *Aside* Georgetown, and at l. 27
     Mr Moses Tickell, Georgetown, Crewe B (Mr.—   F Court, Lord C, Buck)
 8 *bought it of Mr Joseph* Joseph, as the elder son, would have inherited it.

TRIP

Yes, yes, sir; he knows you are here. I did not forget little
Premium. No, no, no.

SIR OLIVER

Very well. And I pray, sir, what may be your name?

TRIP

Trip, sir. My name is Trip, at your service.   20

SIR OLIVER

Well, then, Mr Trip, you have a pleasant sort of place here, I
guess?

TRIP

Why, yes. Here are three or four of us pass our time agreeably
enough, but then our wages are sometimes a little in arrear—
and not very great, either. But fifty pounds a year, and find our   25
own bags and bouquets.

SIR OLIVER

(*Aside*) Bags and bouquets! Halters and bastinadoes!

TRIP

And *à propos*, Moses, have you been able to get me that little
bill discounted?

SIR OLIVER

[*Aside*] Wants to raise money too—mercy on me! Has his distresses   30
too, I warrant, like a lord—and affects creditors and duns.

MOSES

'Twas not to be done, indeed, Mr Trip.   *Gives the note*

TRIP

Good lack, you surprise me! My friend Brush has endorsed it,

17–18 *little Premium* First of many occasions on which he is 'little'. The original Sir Oliver,
       Richard Yates, was a small man, once referred to as 'this dwarfish manager'; see Philip
       H. Highfill Jr. et al., *A Biographical Dictionary of Actors … in London, 1660–1800*
       (1973–93).
   21 *place* employment
   26 *bags* 'an ornamental purse of silk tied to men's hair' (Johnson's *Dictionary*)
       bouquets referring to the fashion among fops to carry 'an immense *bouquet*', Price,
       p. 395. In Foote's *The Nabob* the nouveau riche Nabob is seen choosing flowers for his
       bouquet. Trip aims at the heights of fashion.
   27 *bastinadoes* beatings, especially on the soles of the feet
   29 *bill discounted* 'Promissory note with commission deducted when cashed.' (Bateson)
30–1 *Has his distresses too* Tickell, Murray (Has his distresses   MSS). This addition empha-
       sizes that Trip's thorough aping of his betters reaches to their financial troubles.
   32 s.d. *Gives the note* Lord C, Georgetown, Buck (*pocket book* 1779, not in Tickell)

and I thought when he put his name at the back of a bill 'twas
the same as cash.   35

MOSES

No, 'twouldn't do.

TRIP

A small sum—but twenty pounds. Hark'ee, Moses, do you
think you couldn't get it me by way of annuity?

SIR OLIVER

[*Aside*] An annuity! Ha, ha! A footman raise money by way of
annuity! Well done, luxury, egad!   40

MOSES

Well, but you must insure your place.

TRIP

Oh, with all my heart! I'll insure my place, and my life too, if
you please.

SIR OLIVER

[*Aside*] It's more than I would your neck.

MOSES

But is there nothing you could deposit?   45

34 *name* Tickell, Murray (mark   MSS)

35 *the same as cash* Tickell, Murray (as good as cash   MSS)

38 *annuity* loan, with interest due annually; compare I.i.326.

39 1779 has s.d. *music ready*, a cue for the off-stage accompaniment of the song in III.iii.

40 *luxury, egad!* Tickell, some MSS (egad! MOSES Who would you get to join with you? TRIP
You know my Lord Applicit? You have seen him, however? MOSES Yes. TRIP Very well.
You must have observed what an appearance he makes. Nobody dresses better; nobody
throws off faster. Very well—his own gentleman will stand my security.   F Court,
Lord C)

44 *neck.* Tickell, F Court, Crewe B, Murray, Scott (neck. TRIP But then, Moses, it must be
done before this d——d register takes place—one wouldn't like to have one's name
made public, you know. MOSES No, certainly. Lord C, Georgetown, Buck).
Presumably these lines, referring to the 1777 Annuity Act's requiring all annuities to be
registered, were cut when no longer topical.

TRIP

Why, nothing capital of my master's wardrobe has dropped lately; but I could give you a mortgage on some of his winter clothes, with equity of redemption before November. Or you shall have the reversion of the French velvet, or a post obit on the blue and silver. These, I should think, Moses, with a few pair of point ruffles, is a collateral security—hey, my little fellow?   50

MOSES

Well, well.   *Bell rings*

TRIP

Egad, I heard the bell. I believe, gentlemen, I can now introduce you. Don't forget the annuity, little Moses! This way, gentlemen. Insure my place, you know.   55

SIR OLIVER

If the man be a shadow of the master, this is the temple of dissipation indeed.

Exeunt

Act III, Scene iii

CHARLES SURFACE, CARELESS, GENTLEMEN COMPANIONS
at a table with wine, etc.

CHARLES

'Fore Heaven, 'tis true—here is the great degeneracy of the age! Many of our acquaintance have taste, spirit, and politeness; but plague on't they won't drink.

CARELESS

It is so, indeed, Charles. They give in to all the substantial

46–51 *capital ... collateral security* Trip, speaking of raising money on his master's 'dropped' clothes, demonstrates complete familiarity with the gentlemanly art of borrowing money, and its terminology, including, in the omitted passage quoted at l. 40, relying on the credit of one's friends.

49 *reversion* 'a sum which falls to be paid on the death of a person' (*OED* I.1. d), to be paid here on the passing on of Charles's coat
post obit bond securing a loan on the borrower's expectations at the death of a another person; compare III.iii.157–8.

51 *point ruffles* frills, edged with 'point' lace, worn at the wrist
is Tickell, Lord C, Georgetown (as   F Court, Crewe B, Buck, Bateson)

0 s.d. The 'Chamber' of the previous scene is raised to reveal Charles and his friends; their number and names vary in the MSS. 'Antique Hall. Table covered with green cloth, two decanters of wine, plenty of glasses, two chairs. Charles, Careless and 4 gents discovered at a table, drinking' (Scott).

luxuries of the table, and abstain from nothing but wine and   5
wit.

CHARLES

Oh, certainly, society suffers by it intolerably. For now, instead
of the social spirit of raillery that used to mantle over a glass of
bright burgundy, their conversation is become just like the Spa-
water they drink, which has all the pertness and flatulence of   10
champagne, without its spirit or flavour.

1ST GENTLEMAN

But what are they to do who love play better than wine?

CARELESS

True. There's Harry diets himself for gaming, and is now under
a hazard regimen.

CHARLES

Then he'll have the worst of it. What! You wouldn't train a   15
horse for the course by keeping him from corn. For my part,
egad, I am now never so successful as when I am a little merry.
Let me throw on a bottle of champagne, and I never lose—at
least I never feel my losses, which is exactly the same thing.

2ND GENTLEMAN

Aye, that I believe.   20

CHARLES

And then, what man can pretend to be a believer in love, who
is an abjurer of wine? 'Tis the test by which the lover knows his
own heart. Fill a dozen bumpers to a dozen beauties, and she
that floats atop is the maid that has bewitched you.

CARELESS

Now then, Charles, be honest, and give us your real favourite.   25

CHARLES

Why, I have withheld her only in compassion to you. If I toast
her, you must give a round of her peers, which is impossible—
on earth.

---

   7 s.p. CHARLES MSS (not in Tickell); Tickell makes this speech a continuation of
      Careless's.
  12 *play* gaming, gambling
  14 *hazard* game of dice
  18 *throw* i.e. throw the dice
  23 *bumpers* glasses filled to the brim
27–8 *impossible—on earth* Tickell (impossible (*sighs*) on earth   1779)

CARELESS

Oh, then we'll find some canonized vestals or heathen god-
desses that will do, I warrant.   30

CHARLES

Here then, bumpers, you rogues! Bumpers! Maria! Maria!   *Drink*

1ST GENTLEMAN

Maria who?

CHARLES

Oh, damn the surname! 'Tis too formal to be registered in
love's calendar. But now, Sir Harry, beware! We must have
beauty's superlative.   35

CARELESS

Nay, never study, Sir Harry. We'll stand to the toast though
your mistress should want an eye, and you know you have a
song will excuse you.

SIR HARRY

Egad, so I have, and I'll give him the song instead of the lady.

SONG AND CHORUS

> Here's to the maiden of bashful fifteen;   40
> Here's to the widow of fifty;
> Here's to the flaunting, extravagant quean,
> And here's to the housewife that's thrifty.

> CHORUS   Let the toast pass,
>   Drink to the lass,   45

29   *canonized vestals* virgin saints

31   *Maria! Drink* Georgetown (Maria!   Tickell; Maria. (*sighs*)   1779)

32   s.p. *1ST GENTLEMAN* Tickell, MSS. Bateson, following Georgetown, has SIR TOBY here
(and at ll. 34, 36 and 39 s.p.) but the singer is not necessarily the speaker of this line.

34   *Sir Harry* Tickell, Crewe B, Buck, 1779 (Sir Toby Bumper   Georgetown; Careless F
Court, Lord C). In each MS, the same name appears in Careless's, or 1ST GENTLEMAN's
next speech (l. 36).

39   s.p. *SIR HARRY* Tickell, Crewe B, Buck (CARELESS   F Court, Lord C; SIR TOBY
Georgetown, Bateson)

40   The song echoes 'A Health to the nut-brown lass' in *The Goblins* (1638) by Sir John
Suckling, whose *Works* had appeared in a new edition in 1770. It became a highlight of
the play: a 1780 playbill announces 'In Act III a song by Mr Vernon', a well-known
Drury Lane actor and singer. The music was by Thomas Linley, Sheridan's father-in-
law. When the music for the musical entertainment *The Camp*, another Sheridan-
Linley collaboration, was published in 1778, this 'favourite song in the School for
Scandal' appeared again.

42   *quean* bold, impudent young woman, a hussy (*OED* quotes this line)

I'll warrant she'll prove an excuse for the glass!

Here's to the charmer whose dimples we prize;
Now to the maid who has none, sir!
Here's to the girl with a pair of blue eyes,
And here's to the nymph with but *one*, sir!   50

CHORUS   Let the toast pass, etc.

Here's to the maid with a bosom of snow!
Now to her that's brown as a berry!
Here's to the wife with a face full of woe,
And now to the girl that is merry!   55

CHORUS   Let the toast pass, etc.

For let 'em be clumsy, or let 'em be slim,
Young or ancient, I care not a feather.
So fill a pint bumper quite up to the brim,
And let us e'en toast them together!   60

CHORUS   Let the toast pass, etc.

ALL
Bravo! Bravo!

TRIP *enters and whispers* CHARLES

CHARLES
Gentlemen, you must excuse me a little. Careless, take the chair, will you?

CARELESS
Nay, prithee, Charles, what now? This is one of your peerless   65
beauties, I suppose, has dropped in by chance?

CHARLES
No, faith! To tell you the truth, 'tis a Jew and a broker, who are come by appointment.

CARELESS
Oh, damn it, let's have the Jew in.

---

55 *And now to the girl that is merry* Tickell, Murray (For the damsel that's merry   MSS);
    girl suits the tone of the song better than 'damsel'.
67 *a Jew and a broker* Charles makes a wrong assumption: the money lender, Mr
    Premium, is a Christian. The broker, Moses, is a Jew.

1ST GENTLEMAN

Aye, and the broker too, by all means.   70

2ND GENTLEMAN

Yes, yes, the Jew and the broker!

CHARLES

Egad, with all my heart! Trip, bid the gentlemen walk in—

[*Exit* TRIP]

though there's one of them a stranger, I can tell you.

CARELESS

Charles, let us give them some generous burgundy and perhaps
they'll grow conscientious.   75

CHARLES

Oh, hang 'em, no! Wine does but draw forth a man's natural
qualities, and to make them drink would only be to whet their
knavery.

Enter TRIP, SIR OLIVER [SURFACE], *and* MOSES

So, honest Moses, walk in, walk in, pray, Mr Premium.
That's the gentleman's name, isn't it, Moses?   80

MOSES

Yes, sir.

CHARLES

Set chairs, Trip. Sit down, Mr Premium. Glasses, Trip. Sit
down, Moses. Come, Mr Premium, I'll give you a sentiment.
Here's 'Success to usury'. Moses, fill the gentleman a bumper.

MOSES

'Success to usury'.   [*Drinks*]   85

CARELESS

Right, Moses! Usury is prudence and industry, and deserves to
succeed.

SIR OLIVER

Then—here's 'All the success it deserves!'   [*Drinks*]

75 *they'll grow conscientious* i.e. their consciences will began to trouble them
83 *sentiment* here, a slogan for a toast; for a play on this meaning and 'sentiments' as elev-
    ated, moral feelings, see Frances Sheridan, *A Journey to Bath*. II.i., p. 174: LADY FILMOT
    Do you understand sentiments? EDWARD Oh yes ma'am, I have drunk sentiments very
    often; we give them for toasts.
88 *deserves* Tickell (deserves. CHARLES Mr Premium, you and I are but strangers yet but I
    hope we shall be better acquainted by and by. SIR OLIVER Yes sir, I hope we shall—
    (*Aside*) more intimate perhaps than you'll wish.   F Court, Lord C). Charles's polite
    remark to Premium and Sir Oliver's heavy irony interrupt the comedy of making Sir
    Oliver pay the penalty for his bad form in changing the sentiment of the toast.

CARELESS
No, no, that won't do. Mr Premium, you have demurred at the
toast and must drink it in a pint bumper.   90

1ST GENTLEMAN
A pint bumper at least.

MOSES
Oh pray sir, consider. Mr Premium's a gentleman.

CARELESS
And therefore loves good wine.

2ND GENTLEMAN
Give Moses a quart glass. This is mutiny and a high contempt
for the chair.   95

CARELESS
Here, now for't. I'll see justice done to the last drop of my bottle.

SIR OLIVER
Nay, pray, gentlemen. I did not expect this usage.

CHARLES
No, hang it, you shan't. Mr Premium's a stranger.

SIR OLIVER
Odd! I wish I was well out of their company.

CARELESS
Plague on 'em then! If they don't drink, we'll not sit down with 'em.   100
Come, Harry, the dice are in the next room. Charles, you'll join us
when you have finished your business with these gentlemen?

CHARLES
I will! I will!

Exeunt [CARELESS *and* COMPANIONS]

Careless!

[*Enter* CARELESS]

CARELESS
Well?   105

CHARLES
Perhaps I may want you.

CARELESS
Oh, you know I am always ready: word, note or bond, 'tis all
the same to me.   *Exit*

89 *demurred at* taken exception to, i.e. by changing the words of the toast
100 *don't drink* Tickell, Murray (won't drink   MSS)
108 s.d. *Exit* Georgetown (*Exit Careless*   Buck)

MOSES

Sir, this is Mr Premium, a gentleman of the strictest honour and secrecy—and always performs what he undertakes. Mr   110 Premium, this is—

CHARLES

Pshaw! Have done. Sir, my friend Moses is a very honest fellow, but a little slow at expression. He'll be an hour giving us our titles. Mr Premium, the plain state of the matter is this: I am an extravagant young fellow who want money to borrow, you I   115 take to be a prudent old fellow who have got money to lend. I am blockhead enough to give fifty per cent sooner than not have it, and you, I presume, are rogue enough to take a hundred if you can get it. Now, sir, you see we are acquainted at once and may proceed to business without further   120 ceremony.

SIR OLIVER

Exceeding frank, upon my word. I see, sir, you are not a man of many compliments.

CHARLES

Oh, no, sir. Plain dealing in business I always think best.

SIR OLIVER

Sir, I like you the better for it. However, you are mistaken in   125 one thing. I have no money to lend, but I believe I could procure some of a friend. But then he's an unconscionable dog, isn't he Moses?

MOSES

But you can't help that.

SIR OLIVER

And must sell stock to accommodate you—mustn't he,   130 Moses?

---

115 *want money to borrow* Tickell, MSS, 1779, Scott (wants to borrow money   Murray, Bateson). Price (p. 5) explains how this colloquial phrase results from a Sheridan correction in an early draft: 'to borrow', an addition, was mistakenly taken to be inserted after, instead of before, 'money'. Murray (1821) makes the correction, but before then promptbooks, and a 1792 newspaper comment complaining about the 'uncouth phrase', testify to its being spoken.

116 *prudent* in contrast to *extravagant,* but compare more disparaging uses of *prudence*: l. 86, II.iii.75–7.

127–31 *But . . . Moses* Tickell (But then he's an unconscionable dog, isn't he Moses? And must sell stock to accommodate you—mustn't he, Moses? MSS). Tickell makes the most of Sir Oliver's attempt to repeat the lines the audience heard Moses give him (III.i.98–105), including Moses' prompt: *But you can't help that.*

MOSES

    Yes, indeed! You know I always speak the truth, and I scorn to
    tell a lie!

CHARLES

    Right. People that expect truth generally do: but these are
    trifles, Mr Premium. What! I know money isn't to be bought   135
    without paying for't.

SIR OLIVER

    Well—but what security could you give? You have no land, I
    suppose?

CHARLES

    Not a mole-hill, nor a twig, but what's in the beau-pot out of
    the window!   140

SIR OLIVER

    Nor any stock, I presume?

CHARLES

    Nothing but live-stock—and that's only a few pointers and
    ponies. But pray, Mr Premium, are you acquainted at all with
    any of my connections?

SIR OLIVER

    Why, to say truth, I am.   145

CHARLES

    Then you must know that I have a dev'lish rich uncle in the
    East Indies, Sir Oliver Surface, from whom I have the greatest
    expectations.

SIR OLIVER

    That you have a wealthy uncle I have heard, but how your
    expectations will turn out is more, I believe, than you can tell.   150

CHARLES

    Oh, no. There can be no doubt. They tell me I'm a prodigious
    favourite and that he talks of leaving me everything.

SIR OLIVER

    Indeed! This is the first I've heard on't.

CHARLES

    Yes, yes, 'tis just so. Moses knows 'tis true, don't you, Moses?

MOSES

    Oh, yes! I'll swear to't.   155

139–40 *in the beau-pot out of the window* Tickell (in beau pots out of (at) the window   MSS)
     beau-pot (sp. 'Bow Pot' in Tickell) bough-pot, large vessel for holding cut branches
  144 *connections* relatives
  151 *doubt* Tickell, MSS, Murray (doubt of it Crewe B in Sheridan's hand)

SIR OLIVER

[*Aside*] Egad, they'll persuade me presently I'm at Bengal.

CHARLES

Now I propose, Mr Premium, if it's agreeable to you, a post obit on Sir Oliver's life, though at the same time the old fellow has been so liberal to me that I give you my word I should be very sorry to hear that anything had happened to him.   160

SIR OLIVER

Not more than I should, I assure you. But the bond you mention happens to be just the worst security you could offer me—for I might live to a hundred and never see the principal.

CHARLES

Oh, yes, you would. The moment Sir Oliver dies, you know, you would come on me for the money.   165

SIR OLIVER

Then I believe I should be the most unwelcome dun you ever had in your life.

CHARLES

What? I suppose you are afraid now that Sir Oliver is too good a life?

SIR OLIVER

No, indeed I am not—though I have heard he is as hale and healthy as any man of his years in Christendom.   170

CHARLES

There again you are misinformed. No, no, the climate has hurt him considerably, poor Uncle Oliver. Yes, yes, he breaks apace, I'm told—and so much altered lately, that his nearest relations don't know him.

SIR OLIVER

No? Ha, ha, ha!—so much altered lately, that his nearest   175
relations don't know him! Ha, ha, ha! Egad. Ha, ha, ha!

CHARLES

Ha, ha! You're glad to hear that, little Premium.

SIR OLIVER

No, no, I'm not.

157–8 *a post obit* Tickell, Murray (to grant you a post obit   MSS). For post obit, see note at
          III.ii.49.

  163 *see* Tickell (recover   MSS, Bateson)

  168 *too good a life* i.e. likely to live too long

  172 *breaks apace* his health is failing fast

  176 *Egad* Tickell, Murray, Crewe B (That's droll, egad   MSS)

CHARLES

Yes, yes, you are. Ha, ha, ha! You know that mends your chance.

SIR OLIVER

But I am told Sir Oliver is coming over. Nay, some say he is   180
actually arrived.

CHARLES

Pshaw! Sure I must know better than you whether he's come or not.
No, no, rely on't, he is at this moment at Calcutta, isn't he, Moses?

MOSES

Oh, yes, certainly.

SIR OLIVER

Very true, as you say, you must know better than I, though I   185
have it from pretty good authority, haven't I, Moses?

MOSES

Yes, most undoubted!

SIR OLIVER

But, sir, as I understand you want a few hundreds immediately,
is there nothing you could dispose of?

CHARLES

How do you mean?   190

SIR OLIVER

For instance now, I have heard that your father left behind him
a great quantity of massy old plate.

CHARLES

Oh, lud, that's gone, long ago. Moses can tell you how, better
than I can.

SIR OLIVER

(*Aside*) Good lack, all the family race-cups and corporation   195
bowls! – Then it was also supposed that his library was one of
the most valuable and complete.

CHARLES

Yes, yes, so it was—vastly too much so for a private
gentleman. For my part, I was always of a communicative
disposition; so I thought it a shame to keep so much   200
knowledge to myself.

SIR OLIVER

[*Aside*] Mercy on me! Learning that had run in the family like
an heirloom! – Pray what are become of the books?

___

195 s.d. *Aside* Georgetown, Crewe B, both in Sheridan's hand

CHARLES

You must inquire of the auctioneer, Master Premium, for I
don't believe even Moses can direct you.   205

MOSES

I know nothing of books.

SIR OLIVER

So, so, nothing of the family property left, I suppose?

CHARLES

Not much, indeed, unless you have a mind to the family
pictures. I have got a room full of ancestors above; and if you
have a taste for paintings, egad, you shall have 'em a bargain.   210

SIR OLIVER

Hey! And the devil! Sure, you wouldn't sell your forefathers,
would you?

CHARLES

Every man of them to the best bidder.

SIR OLIVER

What! Your great-uncles and aunts?

CHARLES

Aye, and my great-grandfathers and grandmothers too.   215

SIR OLIVER

(*Aside*) Now I give him up! – What the plague, have you no
bowels for your own kindred? Odd's life, do you take me for
Shylock in the play that you would raise money of me on your
own flesh and blood?

---

206 *I know nothing of books* Tickell, Murray (I never meddle with books   Buck,
     Georgetown, Crewe B)
208 Charles has none of the petty pride of Sir Jeremy in Frances Sheridan's *A Journey to
     Bath*, III.xi, p. 196: 'SIR JEREMY ... If I had your ladyship at Bull-hall, I could shew you
     a line of Ancestry, that would convince you we are not people of yesterday. EDWARD
     Pray Uncle, how came it that you never shewd them to me? SIR JEREMY Why the land
     and the Mansion house has slipp'd thro' our fingers, boy; but thank heaven the family
     pictures are still extant. LADY FILMOT That's a great consolation, Sir Jeremy!'
210 *paintings* Tickell, Murray (old paintings   MSS)
216 s.d. *Aside* Georgetown in Sheridan's hand
216–17 *no bowels for* no feeling for; traditional psychology identified 'the bowels' as the seat of
     compathy, sympathy, etc.
218–19 *Shylock ... blood* As Antonio borrows from Shylock on the surety of a pound of his own
     flesh, so Charles, borrowing of Mr Premium, will offer his own family pictures as surety.
     The Merchant of Venice was the most frequently performed Shakespearean comedy at
     this time, thanks largely to Charles Macklin's revolutionary tragic portrayal of Shylock
     (1740). Thomas King (Sir Peter) had played Shylock in the 1775–6 Drury Lane season.

CHARLES

Nay, my little broker, don't be angry. What need you care if   220
you have your money's worth?

SIR OLIVER

Well, I'll be the purchaser. I think I can dispose of the family
canvas. [*Aside*] Oh, I'll never forgive him this—never.

Enter CARELESS

CARELESS

Come, Charles; what keeps you?

CHARLES

I can't come yet. I'faith, we are going to have a sale above.   225
Here's little Premium will buy all my ancestors.

CARELESS

Oh, burn your ancestors!

CHARLES

No, he may do that afterwards if he pleases. Stay, Careless, we
want you. Egad, you shall be auctioneer; so come along with us.

CARELESS

Oh, have with you, if that's the case. I can handle a hammer as   230
well as a dice-box.

SIR OLIVER

Oh, the profligates!

CHARLES

Come, Moses, you shall be appraiser if we want one. Gad's life,
little Premium, you don't seem to like the business.

SIR OLIVER

Oh, yes, I do, vastly. Ha, ha, ha! Yes, yes, I think it a rare joke   235
to sell one's family by auction. Ha, ha! [*Aside*] Oh, the prodigal!

CHARLES

To be sure! When a man wants money, where the plague should
he get assistance if he can't make free with his own relations?

Exeunt

222–3 *family canvas* Tickell, MSS, Murray (family   Georgetown). 'Tickell and Murray revert
to the less offensive reading' (Bateson).

225 *above* Tickell, MSS (above stairs   Murray)

227 *burn* to hell with

o s.d. 1 Portraits appeared on de Loutherbourg's back flat, some matching those mentioned by Charles. 'Settee on. Great chair ready to bring on. Pedigree hung up first
wing. Pocketbook [i.e. wallet] for Sir Oliver, pocketbook and pencil for Moses.' (Scott)

Act IV, Scene i

Picture room at CHARLES*'s*
Enter CHARLES [SURFACE], SIR OLIVER [SURFACE], MOSES *and*
CARELESS

CHARLES

Walk in, gentlemen, pray walk in. Here they are, the family of the Surfaces, up to the Conquest.

SIR OLIVER

And, in my opinion, a goodly collection.

CHARLES

Aye, aye, these are done in the true spirit of portrait painting— no volunteer grace and expression, not like the works of your 5 modern Raphael, who gives you the strongest resemblance, yet contrives to make your own portrait independent of you, so that you may sink the original and not hurt the picture. No, no, the merit of these is the inveterate likeness—all stiff and awkward as the originals, and like nothing in human nature beside. 10

SIR OLIVER

Ah! we shall never see such figures of men again.

CHARLES

I hope not. Well, you see, Master Premium, what a domestic character I am. Here I sit of an evening surrounded by my family. But come, get to your pulpit, Mr Auctioneer. Here's an old gouty chair of my grandfather's will answer the purpose. 15

CARELESS

Aye, aye, this will do. But, Charles, I have ne'er a hammer— and what's an auctioneer without his hammer?

---

2 *up to the Conquest* i.e. back to the Conquest

5–8 *no volunteer ... picture* Contrasting 'inveterate' likenesses with Reynolds' portraits where the figures, though recognizable, were remarkable also for their gracefulness and force of expression.

5 *volunteer* (*volontier* Tickell) voluntary, so gracefulness freely given (by the painter)

5–6 Sheridan assumes his audience would at once recognize Reynolds by this phrase. Reynolds was a friend of Sheridan and his wife, and painted portraits of them both.

8 *sink* conceal

12 *I hope not. Well, you see* Tickell (No, I hope not, you see   Crewe B in Sheridan's hand)

15 *gouty chair* i.e. chair with a leg rest for those suffering from gout

CHARLES

Egad, that's true. What parchment have we here? (*Reading a roll*) Oh, our genealogy in full. Here, Careless, you shall have no common bit of mahogany—here's the family tree for you,   20
you rogue. This shall be your hammer, and now you may knock down my ancestors with their own pedigree.

SIR OLIVER

What an unnatural rogue—an *ex post facto* parricide!

CARELESS

Yes, yes, here's a list of your generation indeed. Faith, Charles, this is the most convenient thing you could have found for the   25
business, for 'twill serve not only as a hammer but a catalogue into the bargain. But come, begin. A-going, a-going, a-going!

CHARLES

Bravo, Careless. Well, here's my great-uncle, Sir Richard Raveline, a marvellous good general in his day, I assure you. He served in all the Duke of Marlborough's wars, and got that cut   30
over his eye at the Battle of Malplaquet. What say you, Mr Premium? Look at him—there's a hero, not cut out of his feathers, as your modern clipped captains are, but enveloped in wig and regimentals, as a general should be. What do you bid?

MOSES

Mr Premium would have *you* speak.   35

CHARLES

Why, then, he shall have him for ten pounds, and I'm sure that's not dear for a staff officer.

18   *here?* Tickell, Murray (here? *Richard, heir to Thomas* MSS, 1779, Bateson). Some
     identify a family joke here, since Richard Sheridan (rarely on good terms with his
     father) was son but not heir to Thomas.
18-19   s.d. *Reading a roll* Crewe B in Sheridan's hand
     23   *ex post facto* acting retrospectively
          parricide Because Charles tells Careless to 'knock them down'.
     24   *list* MSS, Murray (bit   Tickell). A copyist's error.
          generation i.e. genealogy
     29   *Raveline* specific form of fortification
     31   *Malplaquet* (anglicized in Tickell: Malplacket) a battle in the War of the Spanish
          Succession, in 1709, between the French and allied forces under the Duke of
          Marlborough and Prince Eugène of Savoy
     32   *a hero* Tickell, MSS (a hero for you   Georgetown, Bateson)
     32-3   *not cut ... captains are* i.e. he is wearing a plumed hat

SIR OLIVER

Heaven deliver me! His famous uncle Richard for ten pounds! Well, sir, I take him at that.

CHARLES

Careless, knock down my uncle Richard! Here now is a maiden 40 sister of his, my great-aunt Deborah, done by Kneller, thought to be in his best manner, and a very formidable likeness. There she is, you see, a shepherdess feeding her flock. You shall have her for five pounds ten—the sheep are worth the money.

SIR OLIVER

Ah, poor Deborah—a woman who set such a value on herself! 45 Five pound ten—she's mine.

CHARLES

Knock down my aunt Deborah. Here now are two that were a sort of cousins of theirs. You see, Moses, these pictures were done some time ago, when beaux wore wigs, and the ladies their own hair. 50

SIR OLIVER

Yes, truly, head-dresses appear to have been a little lower in those days.

CHARLES

Well, take that couple for the same.

MOSES

'Tis good bargain.

CHARLES

Careless! This now is a grandfather of my mother's, a learned 55 judge, well known on the western circuit. What do you rate him at, Moses?

MOSES

Four guineas.

41 *Kneller* Sir Godfrey Kneller (1646–1723), German born portrait painter who came to England in 1676 and was from 1689 official court painter, painting 'many ladies in landscapes and pastoral settings, but not as shepherdesses.' (Bateson)

49–50 *when beaux ... hair* In 1777 gentlemen of fashion (*beaux*) wore their own hair powdered, and ladies wore high wigs.

51 *head-dresses ... lower* a comic understatement of the current fashion; Garrick's Prologue to Sheridan's *A Trip to Scarborough* comments on changing fashions, and ridicules the height of ladies' wigs (ll. 38–41) (Price, p. 571): No head of old, too high in feather'd state, / Hinder'd the fair to pass the lowest gate; / A church to enter now, they must be bent, / If ev'r they should try th'experiment.

[112]

CHARLES

Four guineas! Gad's life, you don't bid me the price of his wig. Mr Premium, you have more respect for the woolsack. Do let   60
us knock his lordship down at fifteen.

SIR OLIVER

By all means.

CARELESS

Gone.

CHARLES

And these are two brothers of his, William and Walter Blunt, Esquires, both Members of Parliament and noted speakers; and   65
what's very extraordinary, I believe this is the first time they were ever bought and sold.

SIR OLIVER

That is very extraordinary, indeed! I'll take them at your own price for the honour of Parliament.

CARELESS

Well said, little Premium. I'll knock them down at forty.   70

CHARLES

Here's a jolly fellow. I don't know what relation, but he was Mayor of Manchester. Take him at eight pounds.

SIR OLIVER

No, no; six will do for the Mayor.

CHARLES

Come, make it guineas, and I'll throw you the two aldermen there into the bargain.   75

SIR OLIVER

They're mine.

CHARLES

Careless, knock down the Lord Mayor and aldermen. But, plague on't, we shall be all day retailing in this manner. Do let us deal wholesale, what say you, little Premium? Give us three hundred pounds for the rest of the family in the lump.   80

60 *woolsack* the official seat of the Lord Chancellor in the House of Lords, but here meaning the judiciary
67 *ever bought* i.e. they had never taken bribes
72 *Manchester* Tickell, Georgetown, Murray. In other MSS the name is Bristol, or Norwich: companies playing outside London would vary the name to suit their audience.
79 *Give us* Tickell, Murray (Give me MSS)
80 *for the rest of the family* Tickell, Lord C, Georgetown (and take all that remains on each side   Crewe B, Buck). That is, leaving Sir Oliver's portrait in the middle.

CARELESS

Aye, aye, that will be the best way.

SIR OLIVER

Well, well, anything to accommodate you. They are mine. But there is one portrait which you have always passed over.

CHARLES

What, that ill-looking little fellow over the settee?

SIR OLIVER

Yes, sir, I mean that, though I don't think him so ill-looking a little fellow by any means. 85

CHARLES

What, that? Oh, that's my uncle Oliver. 'Twas done before he went to India.

CARELESS

Your uncle Oliver! Gad, then you'll never be friends, Charles. That now to me is as stern a looking rogue as ever I saw—an unforgiving eye and a damned disinheriting countenance. An inveterate knave, depend on't, don't you think so, little Premium? 90

SIR OLIVER

Upon my soul, sir, I do not. I think it is as honest a looking face as any in the room, dead or alive. But I suppose Uncle Oliver goes with the rest of the lumber? 95

CHARLES

No, hang it! I'll not part with poor Noll. The old fellow has been very good to me, and egad I'll keep his picture while I've a room to put it in.

SIR OLIVER

(*Aside*) The rogue's my nephew after all! – But, sir, I have somehow taken a fancy to that picture. 100

CHARLES

I'm sorry for't, for you certainly will not have it. Oons, haven't you got enough of them?

SIR OLIVER

(*Aside*) I forgive him everything! – But sir, when I take a whim

---

84 *over the settee* Tickell, Murray, MSS (over the door   Lord C). A change probably made to fit the scenery and stage furniture, as with 'on each side', l. 80 above.

95 *Uncle* Tickell, Murray (your Uncle MSS)

100 s.d. *Aside* Georgetown, Crewe B, both in Sheridan's hand

104 s.d. *Aside* Georgetown, in Sheridan's hand, also l. 109

in my head, I don't value money. I'll give as much for that as   105
for all the rest.

CHARLES

Don't tease me, master broker. I tell you I'll not part with it,
and there's an end of it.

SIR OLIVER

(*Aside*) How like his father the dog is! – Well, well, I have done.
(*Aside*) I did not perceive it before, but I think I never saw such   110
a striking resemblance. – Here is a draft for your sum.

CHARLES

Why, 'tis for eight hundred pounds!

SIR OLIVER

You will not let Sir Oliver go?

CHARLES

Zounds, no! I tell you once more.

SIR OLIVER

Then never mind the difference, we'll balance that another time.   115
But give me your hand on the bargain. You are an honest fellow,
Charles. I beg pardon, sir, for being so free. Come, Moses.

CHARLES

Egad, this is a whimsical old fellow! But hark'ee Premium,
you'll prepare lodgings for these gentlemen?

SIR OLIVER

Yes, yes, I'll send for them in a day or two.   120

CHARLES

But hold! Do, now, send a genteel conveyance for them, for, I
assure you, they were most of them used to ride in their own
carriages.

SIR OLIVER

I will, I will—for all but Oliver.

CHARLES

Aye, all but the little nabob.   125

---

110 s.d. *Aside* Buck
111 *striking* Tickell (not in MSS)
125 *little* Tickell (little honest   MSS)
     nabob An official of the East India Company who has made a great fortune while in
     India: though used here without negative overtones, the reputation of the nabob was
     sinking fast. Foote's comedy *The Nabob* mocks the gross, nouveau riche behaviour of
     the returned nabob, and censures his means of enriching himself at the expense of the
     Indians. The impeachment and long trial of Warren Hasting, governor general of the
     East India Company, on charges of oppression and corruption, began in 1785.

SIR OLIVER

You're fixed on that?

CHARLES

Peremptorily.

SIR OLIVER

A dear extravagant rogue! Good day! Come, Moses. Let me hear now who calls him profligate!

Exeunt SIR OLIVER *and* MOSES

CARELESS

Why, this is the oddest genius of the sort I ever saw.   130

CHARLES

Egad, he's the prince of brokers, I think. I wonder how the devil Moses got acquainted with so honest a fellow. Ha, here's Rowley! Do, Careless, say I'll join the company in a few moments.

CARELESS

I will; but don't let that old blockhead persuade you to squander any of that money on old musty debts, or any such nonsense;   135 for tradesmen, Charles, are the most exorbitant fellows!

CHARLES

Very true, and paying them is only encouraging them.

CARELESS

Nothing else.

CHARLES

Aye, aye, never fear.

[*Exit* CARELESS]

So this was an odd old fellow, indeed! Let me see, two-thirds of   140 this is mine by right—five hundred and thirty odd pounds. 'Fore Heaven! I find one's ancestors are more valuable relations than I took them for! Ladies and gentlemen, your most obedient and very grateful humble servant.

Enter ROWLEY

Ha, old Rowley! Egad, you are just come in time to take leave   145 of your old acquaintance.

---

129   *calls* Tickell (dares call   MSS)

130   *genius* nature, disposition

140–1   *two-thirds ... pounds* A third of the £800 goes to Moses as commission; Sheridan's audience was presumably expected to understand why the sum was reduced.

ROWLEY

Yes, I heard they were a-going. But I wonder you can have such spirits under so many distresses.

CHARLES

Why, there's the point—my distresses are so many, that I can't afford to part with my spirits. But I shall be rich and splenetic   150 all in good time. However, I suppose you are surprised that I am not more sorrowful at parting with so many near relations. To be sure, 'tis very affecting; but, rot 'em, you see they never move a muscle, so why should I?

ROWLEY

There's no making you serious a moment.   155

CHARLES

Yes, faith, I am so now. Here, my honest Rowley, here, get me this changed directly, and take a hundred pounds of it immediately to old Stanley.

ROWLEY

A hundred pounds! Consider only—

CHARLES

Gad's life, don't talk about it! Poor Stanley's wants are pressing,   160 and if you don't make haste, we shall have someone call that has a better right to the money.

ROWLEY

Ah, there's the point! I never will cease dunning you with the old proverb—

CHARLES

'Be just before you're generous', hey? Why, so I would if I   165 could; but Justice is an old lame hobbling beldame, and I can't get her to keep pace with Generosity for the soul of me.

ROWLEY

Yet, Charles, believe me, one hour's reflection—

147   *a-going* Tickell (going   MSS)

150   *splenetic* ill-tempered, as a result of a disorder of the spleen; compare note at I.ii.6 on *gall*.

157   *changed directly* Tickell, MSS (changed   Georgetown, Bateson)

165   *'Be just before you're generous'* This 'old proverb' (found first here) may have become current thanks to this passage. Davies writes of Goldsmith: 'He was more generous than just; like honest Charles, in The School for Scandal, he could not, for the soul of him, make justice keep pace with generosity.' (Davies, II, 168)

166   *beldame* old woman, hag

CHARLES

Aye, aye, it's all very true, but hark'ee, Rowley, while I have, by
Heaven I'll give. So damn your economy, and now for hazard.   170

Exeunt

Act IV, Scene ii

The Parlour [at CHARLES*'s house]*
Enter SIR OLIVER [SURFACE] *and* MOSES

MOSES

Well, sir, I think, as Sir Peter said, you have seen Mr Charles in
high glory; 'tis great pity he's so extravagant.

SIR OLIVER

True, but he would not sell my picture.

MOSES

And loves wine and women so much.

SIR OLIVER

But he would not sell my picture.   5

MOSES

And games so deep.

SIR OLIVER

But he wouldn't sell my picture. Oh, here's Rowley.

Enter ROWLEY

ROWLEY

So, Sir Oliver, I find you have made a purchase.

SIR OLIVER

Yes, yes, our young rake has parted with his ancestors like old
tapestry.   10

ROWLEY

And here has he commissioned me to re-deliver you part of the
purchase-money—I mean, though, in your necessitous
character of old Stanley.

MOSES

Ah, there is the pity of all. He is so damned charitable.

---

1 *as Sir Peter said* i.e. at III.i.67
6 *deep* Compare 'I thought you had determined never to venture on such deep play
again', Frances Sheridan, *The Discovery*, IV.i, p. 85.
9–10 *like old tapestry* For lines in F Court removed from here, see note at V.iii.134–5.

ROWLEY

And I left a hosier and two tailors in the hall, who, I'm sure,   15
won't be paid, and this hundred would satisfy them.

SIR OLIVER

Well, well, I'll pay his debts—and his benevolence too. But now
I am no more a broker and you shall introduce me to the elder
brother as old Stanley.

ROWLEY

Not yet awhile. Sir Peter I know means to call there about this   20
time.

Enter TRIP

TRIP

Oh, gentlemen, I beg pardon for not showing you out; this way.
Moses, a word.

Exeunt [TRIP *and* MOSES]

SIR OLIVER

There's a fellow for you! Would you believe it, that puppy
intercepted the Jew on our coming and wanted to raise money   25
before he got to his master?

ROWLEY

Indeed.

SIR OLIVER

Yes, they are now planning an annuity business. Ah, Master
Rowley, in my days servants were content with the follies of
their masters, when they were worn a little threadbare; but   30
now they have their vices, like their Birthday clothes, with the
gloss on.

Exeunt

Act IV, Scene iii

[JOSEPH] SURFACE *and* SERVANT [*in the*] *library in* SURFACE'*s house*

29–32 *servants ... gloss on* i.e. servants used to be content to practise only pale versions of their
masters' follies, but now their vices are as splendid as their masters'

31 *Birthday clothes* 'The King's official birthday, then in January, marked the height of the
social season' (Bateson) and the time for acquiring splendid new clothes.

0 s.d. 1 New scenery by de Loutherbourg (see p. 19): 'A Library (Discovered) Screen on
... Pembroke table – a book on it. Two chairs before the screen and one chair behind
it' [for Lady Teazle to sit on when hiding] (Scott).

SURFACE

No letter from Lady Teazle?

SERVANT

No, sir.

SURFACE

I am surprised she has not sent, if she is prevented from
coming. Sir Peter certainly does not suspect me. Yet, I wish I
may not lose the heiress, through the scrape I have drawn   5
myself in with the wife; however, Charles's imprudence and
bad character are great points in my favour.

Knocking

SERVANT

Sir, I believe that must be Lady Teazle.

SURFACE

Hold! See whether it is or not before you go to the door; I have
a particular message for you, if it should be my brother.   10

SERVANT

'Tis her ladyship, sir; she always leaves her chair at the
milliner's in the next street.

SURFACE

Stay, stay. Draw that screen before the window—that will do.
My opposite neighbour is a maiden lady of so anxious a temper.

SERVANT *draws the screen, and exit*

I have a difficult hand to play in this affair. Lady Teazle has   15
lately suspected my views on Maria, but she must by no means
be let into that secret—at least, till I have her more in my power.

Enter LADY TEAZLE

LADY TEAZLE

What! Sentiment in soliloquy now? Have you been very

---

7   s.d. *Knocking,* or (*Knock*) MSS (not in Tickell)

14 *anxious* Tickell, Murray (curious   MSS). The change avoids the possible ambiguity of
    'curious'.

17 *at least, till I* Tickell, MSS (at least not till I   Crewe B in Sheridan's hand). Bateson
    prefers Crewe B: 'the extra emphasis ... is certainly an improvement'.

18 *in soliloquy now* Tickell, Murray (MSS have 'now' after 'impatient' l. 19). The conven-
    tions surrounding the soliloquy by Sheridan's time lay somewhere between the
    Shakespearean which allowed direct audience address, and late nineteenth-century
    naturalism, where some special reason, e.g. madness, justified a soliloquy. Lady Teazle
    hears Surface speaking, in line with the older convention that a character speaking his
    thoughts could be overheard. Later, the soliloquy moved closer to a representation of
    interior speech, or unspoken thought. In Sheridan's time there was some criticism of
    actors who reverted to direct address and played their soliloquies to the audience.

impatient? O lud, don't pretend to look grave. I vow I couldn't
come before.   20

SURFACE

Oh, madam, punctuality is a species of constancy, a very
unfashionable quality in a lady.

LADY TEAZLE

Upon my word, you ought to pity me. Do you know Sir Peter
is grown so ill-tempered to me of late—and so jealous of
Charles too! That's the best of the story, isn't it?   25

SURFACE

(*Aside*) I am glad my scandalous friends keep that up.

LADY TEAZLE

I am sure I wish he would let Maria marry him and then
perhaps he would be convinced; don't you, Mr Surface?

SURFACE

(*Aside*) Indeed I do not. – Oh, certainly, I do. For then my dear
Lady Teazle would also be convinced how wrong her suspicions   30
were of my having any design on the silly girl.

[They]sit

LADY TEAZLE

Well, well, I'm inclined to believe you. But isn't it provoking to
have the most ill-natured things said to one? And there's my
friend Lady Sneerwell has circulated I don't know how many
scandalous tales of me, and all without any foundation too.   35
That's what vexes me.

SURFACE

Aye, madam, to be sure, that is the provoking circumstance—
without foundation. Yes, yes, there's the mortification, indeed;
for, when a scandalous story is believed against one, there

27 *Maria* MSS (her   Tickell). A copyist's error.

31 s.d. *sit* Georgetown

32 *believe you* At this point Spunge MS has two pages of cancelled dialogue in which Lady
    Teazle reveals her jealousy of Maria, and Surface, with 'unexpected chivalry' (Bateson),
    comes to her defence. The cancelled passage is reprinted in Cecil Price, 'The Clare
    Sheridan MSS. in the British Theatre Museum', *Theatre Notebook*, XXIX, 1975, 51–6, 52.

33 *said to one* Tickell, MSS (said of one   Crewe B). There may be some confusion here.
    Presumably Sir Peter, previously 'ill-tempered' (l. 24), makes the 'ill-natured' remarks.
    However 'ill-natured' (like 'said *of* one') better fits the gossiping Lady Sneerwell, but
    'And there's Lady Sneerwell' seems to mark a turn to this vexing person.

35 *scandalous* Tickell, MSS (slanderous   F Court). Sheridan's earliest sketches were
    headed 'The Slanderers'.

certainly is no comfort like the consciousness of having   40
deserved it.

LADY TEAZLE

No, to be sure, then I'd forgive their malice. But to attack me,
who am really so innocent and who never say an ill-natured
thing of anybody—that is, of any friend; and then Sir Peter too,
to have him so peevish, and so suspicious, when I know the   45
integrity of my own heart—indeed, 'tis monstrous!

SURFACE

But, my dear Lady Teazle, 'tis your own fault if you suffer it.
When a husband entertains a groundless suspicion of his wife
and withdraws his confidence from her, the original compact is
broke; and she owes it to the honour of her sex to outwit him.   50

LADY TEAZLE

Indeed! So that, if he suspects me without cause, it follows
that the best way of curing his jealousy is to give him reason
for it?

SURFACE

Undoubtedly—for your husband should never be deceived in
you; and in that case, it becomes you to be frail in compliment   55
to his discernment.

LADY TEAZLE

To be sure, what you say is very reasonable, and when the
consciousness of my own innocence—

SURFACE

Ah, my dear madam, there is the great mistake! 'Tis this very
conscious innocence that is of the greatest prejudice to you.   60
What is it makes you negligent of forms, and careless of the
world's opinion? Why, the consciousness of your own
innocence. What makes you thoughtless in your conduct, and
apt to run into a thousand little imprudences? Why, the
consciousness of your own innocence. What makes you   65
impatient of Sir Peter's temper, and outrageous at his
suspicions? Why, the consciousness of your innocence.

LADY TEAZLE

'Tis very true.

---

50 *broke* Tickell, MSS (broken   Murray, Bateson)
    to outwit Tickell, Murray (to endeavour to outwit   MSS)
66 *outrageous* feel outraged

SURFACE

Now, my dear Lady Teazle, if you would but once make a
trifling *faux pas*, you can't conceive how cautious you would   70
grow, and how ready to humour and agree with your husband.

LADY TEAZLE

Do you think so?

SURFACE

Oh, I'm sure on't; and then you would find all scandal would
cease at once; for, in short, your character at present is like a
person in a plethora, absolutely dying from too much health.   75

LADY TEAZLE

So, so; then I perceive your prescription is that I must sin in my
own defence, and part with my virtue to secure my reputation?

SURFACE

Exactly so, upon my credit, ma'am.

LADY TEAZLE

Well, certainly this is the oddest doctrine, and the newest
receipt for avoiding calumny.   80

SURFACE

An infallible one, believe me. Prudence, like experience, must
be paid for.

LADY TEAZLE

Why, if my understanding were once convinced—

SURFACE

Oh, certainly, madam, your understanding should be
convinced. Yes, yes—Heaven forbid I should persuade you to   85
do anything you *thought* wrong. No, no, I have too much
honour to desire it.

LADY TEAZLE

Don't you think we may as well leave *honour* out of the argument?

SURFACE

Ah, the ill effects of your country education, I see, still remain
with you.   90

---

75 *plethora* unhealthy repletion; originally, medical term for an excess of fluid, especially blood
77 *secure* Tickell, Murray, Crewe B (preserve other MSS). A typical fine distinction, and
    an instance of a variation being carried into Tickell.
88 *argument?* Dublin 1780 has here s.d. *Both rise*
89 *country education* Surface deplores Lady Teazle's moral rebuke, l. 88, and attributes it
    to 'the ill effects' of growing up among country notions of morality. Compare her own
    reference to 'country prejudices', II.ii.231.

LADY TEAZLE

I doubt they do indeed; and I will fairly own to you that if I could be persuaded to do wrong, it would be by Sir Peter's ill usage sooner than your honourable logic after all.

SURFACE

Then by this hand, which he is unworthy of—   *Taking her hand*

Enter SERVANT

'Sdeath, you blockhead—what do you want?   95

SERVANT

I beg your pardon, sir, but I thought you would not choose Sir Peter to come up without announcing him.

SURFACE

Sir Peter! Oons—the devil!

LADY TEAZLE

Sir Peter! O lud, I'm ruined! I'm ruined!

SERVANT

Sir, 'twasn't I let him in.   100

LADY TEAZLE

Oh, I'm quite undone! What will become of me now, Mr Logic? Oh, he's on the stairs. I'll get behind here—and if ever I'm so imprudent again—   *Goes behind the screen*

SURFACE

Give me that book.

Sits down. Servant pretends to adjust his hair

Enter SIR PETER TEAZLE

SIR PETER

Aye, ever improving himself! Mr Surface, Mr Surface—   105

SURFACE

Oh, my dear Sir Peter, I beg your pardon. *(Gaping, and throws away the book)* I have been dozing over a stupid book. Well, I

---

92   *to do wrong* Stating the situation bluntly, and treating ironically his 'honorable logic'.

94   s.d. *Taking her hand* Georgetown, Murray (*Kneeling* Dublin 1780). His line makes it inevitable that he tries to take her hand.

102   *Oh* Tickell, Murray (Oh mercy   MSS)

105   *Mr Surface*— Scott has the s.d. *Taps Joseph on the shoulder* here.

106   s.d. *Gaping* Yawning

106–7   s.d. *throws away the book* Mary, mother of Elizabeth Tickell, wrote to her sister, Elizabeth Sheridan, of a performance in Bath, November 1777: 'I particularly observed that instead of throwing the Book to the other end of the Room as Palmer does he [Dimond] very carefully pulled down the Page he was reading and gave it to his Servant w[hi]ch is certainly more consistent with his Character' (qtd. Price, p. 413).

am much obliged to you for this call. You haven't been here, I
believe, since I fitted up this room. Books, you know, are the
only things I am a coxcomb in.   110

SIR PETER

'Tis very neat indeed. Well, well, that's proper; and you make even
your screen a source of knowledge—hung, I perceive, with maps.

SURFACE

Oh, yes, I find great use in that screen.

SIR PETER

I dare say you must. Certainly when you want to find anything
in a hurry.   115

SURFACE

(*Aside*) Aye, or to hide anything in a hurry either.

SIR PETER

Well, I have a little private business—

SURFACE

(*To* SERVANT) You need not stay.

SERVANT

No, sir.   *Exit*

SURFACE

Here's a chair, Sir Peter, I beg.   120

SIR PETER

Well, now we are alone, there is a subject, my dear friend, on
which I wish to unburden my mind to you—a point of the
greatest moment to my peace; in short, my dear friend, Lady
Teazle's conduct of late has made me extremely unhappy.

SURFACE

Indeed! I am very sorry to hear it.   125

SIR PETER

Aye, 'tis too plain she has not the least regard for me; but,
what's worse, I have pretty good authority to suppose she has
formed an attachment to another.

SURFACE

Indeed! You astonish me!

109–10 *Books ... coxcomb in* 'Books are my only vanity'
116 s.d. *Aside* Crewe B, in Sheridan's hand
118 s.d. *To* SERVANT Georgetown in Sheridan's hand
123 *dear friend* Tickell, Murray (good friend   MSS)
127 *suppose* Tickell, Murray, Buck (suspect   other MSS)
127–8 *has formed* Tickell (must have formed   MSS, Bateson). Possibly a copyist's error.
129 *Indeed* Tickell, Murray, MSS (deleted in Georgetown in Sheridan's hand)

SIR PETER

Yes; and, between ourselves, I think I have discovered the person.   130

SURFACE

How! You alarm me exceedingly.

SIR PETER

Ah, my dear friend, I knew you would sympathize with me!

SURFACE

Yes—believe me, Sir Peter, such a discovery would hurt me just as much as it would you.

SIR PETER

I am convinced of it. Ah, it is a happiness to have a friend   135
whom we can trust even with one's family secrets. But have you no guess who I mean?

SURFACE

I haven't the most distant idea. It can't be Sir Benjamin Backbite?

SIR PETER

Oh, no! What say you to Charles?

SURFACE

My brother! Impossible!   140

SIR PETER

Ah, my dear friend, the goodness of your own heart misleads you. You judge of others by yourself.

SURFACE

Certainly, Sir Peter, the heart that is conscious of its own integrity is ever slow to credit another's treachery.

SIR PETER

True, but your brother has no sentiment. You never hear him   145
talk so.

SURFACE

Yet I can't but think Lady Teazle herself has too much principle.

SIR PETER

Aye, but what's her principle against the flattery of a handsome, lively young fellow?   150

SURFACE

That's very true.

---

136   *we can trust* Tickell (one can trust   MSS, Bateson)
145–6 Sir Peter's comment alludes to Surface's 'sentiment' in the previous speech.
149   *what's her principle* MSS (what's the principle   Tickell; what is principle Bateson). A Tickell copyist's error.

SIR PETER

And then, you know, the difference of our ages makes it very improbable that she should have any very great affection for me; and, if she were to be frail, and I were to make it public, why, the town would only laugh at me—the foolish old bachelor who had married a girl.   155

SURFACE

That's true, to be sure. They would laugh.

SIR PETER

Laugh—aye, and make ballads and paragraphs and the devil knows what of me.

SURFACE

No, you must never make it public.   160

SIR PETER

But then, again, that the nephew of my old friend, Sir Oliver, should be the person to attempt such a wrong, hurts me more nearly.

SURFACE

Aye, there's the point. When ingratitude barbs the dart of injury, the wound has double danger in it.   165

SIR PETER

Aye. I that was, in a manner, left his guardian, in whose house he had been so often entertained—who never in my life denied him my advice!

SURFACE

Oh, 'tis not to be credited! There may be a man capable of such baseness, to be sure; but, for my part, till you can give me positive proofs, I cannot but doubt it. However, if it should be proved on him, he is no longer a brother of mine; I disclaim kindred with him; for the man who can break the laws of hospitality and attempt the wife of his friend, deserves to be branded as the pest of society.   175

SIR PETER

What a difference there is between you. What noble sentiments!

SURFACE

Yet I cannot suspect Lady Teazle's honour.

---

153   *any very great* Tickell, Murray, Buck (a great   Georgetown; any   F Court, Lord C, Crewe B)

173   *break the laws* Tickell, Murray (break through the laws   MSS)

SIR PETER

I am sure I wish to think well of her and to remove all ground
of quarrel between us. She has lately reproached me more than
once with having made no settlement on her, and in our last   180
quarrel she almost hinted that she should not break her heart if
I was dead. Now, as we seem to differ in our ideas of expense, I
have resolved she shall have her own way and be her own
mistress in that respect for the future; and, if I were to die, she
will find that I have not been inattentive to her interest while   185
living. Here, my friend, are the drafts of two deeds, which I
wish to have your opinion on. By one she will enjoy eight
hundred a year independent while I live; and, by the other, the
bulk of my fortune at my death.

SURFACE

This conduct, Sir Peter, is indeed truly generous. (*Aside*) I wish   190
it may not corrupt my pupil.

SIR PETER

Yes, I am determined she shall have no cause to complain,
though I would not have her acquainted with the latter instance
of my affection yet awhile.

SURFACE

(*Aside*) Nor I, if I could help it.   195

SIR PETER

And now, my dear friend, if you please, we will talk over the
situation of your affairs with Maria.

SURFACE

(*Softly*) Oh, no, Sir Peter! Another time, if you please.

SIR PETER

I am sensibly chagrined at the little progress you seem to make
in her affection.   200

SURFACE

(*Softly*) I beg you will not mention it. What are my

---

183 *have her own way and* Tickell, Murray (not in MSS)

187–8 *eight hundred* £800 a year is a generous allowance. Garrick received £500 a year as principal actor at Drury Lane in 1741/2, rising to £600 or £700 in 1743. See Davies, I, 52, and
compare Frances Abington's dress allowance, p. 18.

189 *at my death* Tickell, Murray (after my death   MSS)

195 s.d. *Aside* Lord C, Georgetown

197 *affairs* Tickell, Murray (hopes   MSS). This, and the previous variant, are further good
examples of Tickell's small improvements.

198, 201 s.d. *Softly* MSS, Bateson (not in Tickell)

199 *sensibly* acutely, intensely

disappointments when your happiness is in debate! (*Aside*)
'Sdeath, I shall be ruined every way.

SIR PETER

And though you are so averse to my acquainting Lady Teazle
with your passion for Maria, I'm sure she's not your enemy in   205
the affair.

SURFACE

Pray, Sir Peter, now, oblige me. I am really too much affected
by the subject we have been speaking on, to bestow a thought
on my own concerns. The man who is entrusted with his
friend's distresses can never—   210

Enter SERVANT

Well, sir?

SERVANT

Your brother, sir, is speaking to a gentleman in the street, and
says he knows you are within.

SURFACE

'Sdeath, blockhead—I'm not within. I'm out for the day.

SIR PETER

Stay. Hold. A thought has struck me. You shall be at home.   215

SURFACE

Well, well, let him up.

[*Exit* SERVANT]

[*Aside*] He'll interrupt Sir Peter, however.

SIR PETER

Now, my good friend, oblige me, I entreat you. Before Charles
comes, let me conceal myself somewhere; then do you tax him
on the point we have been talking on, and his answer may   220
satisfy me at once.

SURFACE

Oh, fie, Sir Peter! Would you have me join in so mean a trick—
to trepan my brother too?

SIR PETER

Nay, you tell me you are sure he is innocent; if so, you do him
the greatest service by giving him an opportunity to clear   225

---

202   s.d. *Aside* Georgetown, Crewe B, in Sheridan's hand
205   *passion for Maria* Tickell (passion   MSS)
223   *trepan* trap; compare 'Mr G. I should suppose cannot at present have trepanned you
       into any absolute promise' (*Letters*, III, 294), Sheridan to Thomas Linley on a proposed
       agreement with Garrick (1775).

himself, and you will set my heart at rest. Come, you shall not
refuse me. Here, behind this screen will be— (*Goes to the
screen*) Hey! What the devil! There seems to be one listener
there already. I'll swear I saw a petticoat.

SURFACE

Ha, ha, ha! Well, this is ridiculous enough. I'll tell you, Sir   230
Peter, though I hold a man of intrigue to be a most despicable
character, yet you know it doesn't follow that one is to be an
absolute Joseph either. Hark'ee, 'tis a little French milliner, a
silly rogue that plagues me—and having some character, on
your coming, sir, she ran behind the screen.   235

SIR PETER

Ah, you rogue! But, egad, she has overheard all I have been
saying of my wife.

SURFACE

Oh, 'twill never go any farther, you may depend upon it.

SIR PETER

No? Then i'faith let her hear it out. Here's a closet will do as well.

SURFACE

Well, go in then.   240

SIR PETER

Sly rogue! Sly rogue!   *Going into the closet*

SURFACE

A narrow escape, indeed, and a curious situation I'm in to part
man and wife in this manner.

LADY TEAZLE

(*Peeping*) Couldn't I steal off?

SURFACE

Keep close, my angel.   245

SIR PETER

(*Peeping*) Joseph, tax him home.

---

231   *man of intrigue* man who goes in for secret affairs; compare 'Your unacquaintedness
with men of intrigue makes you blind to your own danger', Frances Sheridan, *The
Discovery*, III.ii, p. 75.

232–3 *an absolute Joseph* Joseph resisted the repeated advances of the wife of his master,
Potifer, Genesis 39. 7–12.

234   *character* reputation, as a respectable woman

241   s.d. *Going into the closet* i.e. through one of the doors in the side of the proscenium, see
illustration, p. 19. Many comedies of the period have scenes using an off stage 'closet':
Sheridan's *A Trip to Scarborough* has three.

SURFACE

Back, my dear friend.

LADY TEAZLE

(*Peeping*) Couldn't you lock Sir Peter in?

SURFACE

Be still, my life.

SIR PETER

(*Peeping*) You're sure the little milliner won't blab?   250

SURFACE

In, in, my good Sir Peter. 'Fore Gad, I wish I had a key to the door.

Enter CHARLES [SURFACE]

CHARLES

Hullo, brother, what has been the matter? Your fellow would not let me up at first. What, have you had a Jew or a wench with you?

SURFACE

Neither, brother, I assure you.   255

CHARLES

But what has made Sir Peter steal off? I thought he had been with you.

SURFACE

He *was* brother, but hearing *you* were coming he did not choose to stay.

CHARLES

What! Was the old gentleman afraid I wanted to borrow money   260
of him?

SURFACE

No, sir. But I am sorry to find, Charles, you have lately given that worthy man grounds for great uneasiness.

CHARLES

Yes, they tell me I do that to a great many worthy men. But how so, pray?   265

SURFACE

To be plain with you, brother, he thinks you are endeavouring to gain Lady Teazle's affections from him.

CHARLES

Who, I? O lud, not I, upon my word. Ha, ha, ha, ha! So the old fellow has found out that he has got a young wife, has he? Or, what is worse, her ladyship has found out she has an old husband? 270

SURFACE

This is no subject to jest on, brother. He who can laugh—

CHARLES

True, true, as you were going to say. Then, seriously, I never had the least idea of what you charge me with, upon my honour.

SURFACE

(*Aloud*) Well, it will give Sir Peter great satisfaction to hear this. 275

CHARLES

To be sure, I once thought the lady seemed to have taken a fancy to me; but, upon my soul, I never gave her the least encouragement. Besides, you know my attachment to Maria.

SURFACE

But sure, brother, even if Lady Teazle had betrayed the fondest partiality for you— 280

CHARLES

Why, look'ee, Joseph, I hope I shall never deliberately do a dishonourable action; but if a pretty woman was purposely to throw herself in my way—and that pretty woman married to a man old enough to be her father—

SURFACE

Well? 285

CHARLES

Why, I believe I should be obliged to borrow a little of your morality. That's all. But brother, do you know now that you surprise me exceedingly by naming *me* with Lady Teazle; for, faith, I always understood you were her favourite.

SURFACE

Oh, for shame, Charles! This retort is foolish. 290

CHARLES

Nay, I swear I have seen you exchange such significant glances—

SURFACE

Nay, nay, sir, this is no jest—

---

270 *what is worse ... an old husband?* Tickell, Murray (what's worse, has her ladyship discovered that she has an old husband?   F Court, Lord C, Georgetown; not in Crewe B, Buck). Perhaps omitted out of delicacy in these presentation copies.

CHARLES

Egad, I'm serious. Don't you remember, one day, when I called here—

SURFACE

Nay, prithee, Charles— 295

CHARLES

And found you together—

SURFACE

Zounds, sir, I insist—

CHARLES

And another time, when your servant—

SURFACE

Brother, brother, a word with you. (*Aside*) Gad, I must stop him.

CHARLES

Informed me, I say, that— 300

SURFACE

Hush! I beg your pardon, but Sir Peter has overheard all we have been saying. I knew you would clear yourself, or I should not have consented.

CHARLES

How, Sir Peter! Where is he?

SURFACE

Softly. There! *Points to the closet* 305

CHARLES

Oh, 'fore Heaven, I'll have him out. Sir Peter, come forth!

SURFACE

No, no—

CHARLES

I say, Sir Peter, come into court. (*Pulls in* SIR PETER) What! My old guardian! What, turn inquisitor and take evidence *incog.*?

SIR PETER

Give me your hand, Charles. I believe I have suspected you 310 wrongfully; but you mustn't be angry with Joseph. 'Twas my plan.

CHARLES

Indeed!

SIR PETER

But I acquit you. I promise you I don't think near so ill of

---

300 *Informed me* MSS (Informed   Tickell). Probably a copyist's error.
309 *incog.* incognito, disguised or, here, concealed

you as I did. What I have heard has given me great
satisfaction.   315

CHARLES

Egad then, 'twas lucky you didn't hear any more, (*Half aside*)
wasn't it, Joseph?

SIR PETER

Ah, you would have retorted on him.

CHARLES

Aye, aye, that was a joke.

SIR PETER

Yes, yes, I know his honour too well.   320

CHARLES

But you might as well have suspected *him* as *me* in this matter
for all that. (*Half aside*) Mightn't he, Joseph?

SIR PETER

Well, well, I believe you.

SURFACE

(*Aside*) Would they were both well out of the room!

Enter SERVANT *and whispers* SURFACE

SIR PETER

And in future, perhaps, we may not be such strangers.   325

Exit SERVANT

SURFACE

Gentlemen, I beg your pardon. I must wait on you downstairs.
Here is a person come on particular business.

---

316   s.d. *Half aside* Georgetown in Sheridan's hand, and at l. 322
318   *retorted on him* given him a sharp reply; compare l. 290; *OED* finds *retort* 'not particu-
        larly common before the nineteenth century'.
324   s.d. *Aside* Buck
        s.d. 2 *Enter* SERVANT ... SURFACE Tickell, F Court, Lord C, Georgetown (*Enter*
        Servant (To Surface) Sir Lady Sneerwell is below and says she will come up   Crewe
        B, Buck). The threatened appearance of Lady Sneerwell, with Surface replying 'Lady
        Sneerwell!—stop her by all means', noted first by Sheridan on a loose sheet in F
        Court, is pursued in Georgetown, Crewe B, Buck. Reverting to the original plot-
        ting, Tickell drops the episode but, from the evidence of promptbooks, it con-
        tinued to be played. But it *is* a distraction from the screen business, and her
        appearance in Act V is more effective if not anticipated by the threat of an appear-
        ance here.
326   *I must wait on you downstairs* i.e. please go to a room downstairs where I shall join you

CHARLES

Well, you can see him in another room. Sir Peter and I have not met a long time, and I have something to say to him.

SURFACE

(*Aside*) They must not be left together. – I'll send this man   330
away and return directly. (*Aside to him*) Sir Peter, not a word of the French milliner.

SIR PETER

I? Not for the world.

Exit SURFACE

Ah, Charles, if you associated more with your brother, one might indeed hope for your reformation. He is a Man of   335
Sentiment. Well, there is nothing in the world so noble as a Man of Sentiment.

CHARLES

Pshaw! He is too moral by half—and so apprehensive of his good name, as he calls it, that I suppose he would as soon let a priest into his house as a girl.   340

SIR PETER

No, no! Come, come, you wrong him. No, no, Joseph is no rake, but he is no such saint either in that respect. (*Aside*) I have a great mind to tell him. We should have a laugh.

CHARLES

Oh, hang him, he's a very anchorite, a young hermit.

SIR PETER

Hark'ee, you must not abuse him. He may chance to hear of it   345
again, I promise you.

CHARLES

Why, you won't tell him?

---

329 *something to say to him* Charles is needed for the rest of the scene: this remark gives him a reason to stay.

330 *send this man* Tickell, F Court, Lord C (send Lady Sneerwell F Court sheet, Georgetown, Crewe B, Buck)

331 s.d. *Aside to him* Crewe B in Sheridan's hand

333 s.d. *Exit* SURFACE Crewe B, Buck (not in Tickell; F Court, Lord C, Georgetown have the exit after 'milliner', l. 332)

342 *no such saint* Tickell, F Court, Crewe B (not such a saint   Georgetown)

342 s.d. *Aside* Georgetown, Crewe B, both in Sheridan's hand

344 *very anchorite, a young hermit* Since Charles claims he has previously found Joseph with Lady Teazle, l. 296, and enters asking if he had had a wench with him, this characterization is comic irony, perhaps to lead Sir Peter on.

SIR PETER

No, but, this way. Egad, I'll tell him. Hark'ee, have you a mind
to have a good laugh at Joseph?

CHARLES

I should like it of all things.   350

SIR PETER

Then, i'faith, we will! (*Aside*) I'll be quit with him for
discovering me. (*Whispers*) He had a girl with him when I
called.

CHARLES

What! Joseph? You jest.

SIR PETER

Hush! (*Whispers*) A little French milliner. And the best of the   355
jest is—she's in the room now.

CHARLES

The devil she is!

SIR PETER

Hush! I tell you.   *Points*

CHARLES

Behind the screen! 'Slife, let's unveil her.

SIR PETER

No, no, he's coming—you shan't indeed.   360

CHARLES

Oh, egad, we'll have a peep at the little milliner.

SIR PETER

Not for the world! Joseph will never forgive me.

CHARLES

I'll stand by you.

SIR PETER

(*Struggling with* CHARLES) Odds, here he is!

351 s.d. *Aside* Georgetown, in Sheridan's hand
      be quit with him pay him back
352 s.d. *Whispers* Crewe B (*Whispering* F Court, Buck)
355 s.d. *Whispers* Crewe B, in Sheridan's hand
364 s.d. *Struggling with* CHARLES Georgetown (*Struggling* Crewe B). One of the play's few
      moments of physical action; compare V.iii.85.
      s.d. 2 CHARLES *throws down the screen* Garrick wrote to Sheridan, 12 May 1777, 'A
      gentleman who is as mad as myself about yᵉ School remark'd, that the characters upon
      the stage at yᵉ falling of the screen stand too long before they speak;—I thought so too
      yᵉ first night:—he said it was the same on yᵉ 2nd, and was remark'd by others;—tho'
      they should be astonished, and a little petrify'd, yet it may be carried to too great a
      length.' (Moore, I, 245, qtd. Bateson)

[JOSEPH] SURFACE *enters just as* CHARLES *throws down the screen*

CHARLES

Lady Teazle—by all that's wonderful!   365

SIR PETER

Lady Teazle—by all that's damnable!

CHARLES

Sir Peter this is one of the smartest French milliners I ever saw.
Egad, you seem all to have been diverting yourselves here at
hide and seek—and I don't see who is out of the secret. Shall I
beg your ladyship to inform me? Not a word! Brother, will you   370
be pleased to explain this matter? What, is morality dumb too?
Sir Peter, though I found you in the dark, perhaps you are not
so now? All mute. Well, though I can make nothing of the affair,
I suppose you perfectly understand one another. So I'll leave
you to yourselves. (*Going*) Brother, I'm sorry to find you have   375
given that worthy man so much uneasiness. Sir Peter, there's
nothing in the world so noble as a Man of Sentiment!   *Exit*

Stand for some time looking at each other

SURFACE

Sir Peter, notwithstanding I confess that appearances are
against me, if you will afford me your patience, I make no
doubt—but I shall explain everything to your satisfaction.   380

SIR PETER

If you please, sir.

SURFACE

The fact is, sir, that Lady Teazle, knowing my pretensions to
your ward, Maria—I say, sir—Lady Teazle, being apprehensive
of the jealousy of your temper—and knowing my friendship to
the family—she, sir, I say—called here—in order that I might   385
explain these pretensions—but on your coming, being
apprehensive—as I said—of your jealousy, she withdrew—and
this, you may depend on it, is the whole truth of the matter.

SIR PETER

A very clear account, upon my word; and I dare swear the lady
will vouch for every article of it.   390

366   *damnable!* Tickell, Murray (horrible!   MSS)
376   *so much* Tickell, Georgetown (grounds for so much   Crewe B, Buck)
382   *pretensions* claims (as a recognized suitor)

LADY TEAZLE

(*Coming forward*) For not one word of it, Sir Peter.

SIR PETER

How? Don't you even think it worth while to agree in the lie?

LADY TEAZLE

There is not one syllable of truth in what that gentleman has told you.

SIR PETER

I believe you, upon my soul, ma'am.   395

SURFACE

(*Aside*) 'Sdeath, madam, will you betray me?

LADY TEAZLE

Good Mr Hypocrite, by your leave, I'll speak for myself.

SIR PETER

Aye, let her alone, sir; you'll find she'll make out a better story than you without prompting.

LADY TEAZLE

Hear me, Sir Peter! I came hither on no matter relating to your   400
ward, and even ignorant of this gentleman's pretensions to her.
But I came seduced by his insidious arguments, at least to listen
to his pretended passion, if not to sacrifice your honour to his
baseness.

SIR PETER

Now I believe the truth is coming indeed!   405

SURFACE

The woman's mad!

LADY TEAZLE

No, sir, she has recovered her senses, and your own arts have
furnished her with the means. Sir Peter, I do not expect you to
credit me, but the tenderness you expressed for me, when I am
sure you could not think I was a witness to it, has penetrated so   410
to my heart that had I left the place without the shame of this
discovery, my future life should have spoke the sincerity of my
gratitude. As for that smooth-tongued hypocrite, who would
have seduced the wife of his too credulous friend, while he
affected honourable addresses to his ward—I behold him now   415

---

391 s.d. *Coming forward* Georgetown in Sheridan's hand, Crewe B, Buck. This suggests that she has stayed up stage, frozen, since she was revealed.

403 *your honour* As the husband was thought to be responsible for the wife's conduct, her infidelity would have meant sacrificing his honour as well as hers.

in a light so truly despicable that I shall never again respect
myself for having listened to him.   *Exit*

SURFACE

Notwithstanding all this, Sir Peter, Heaven knows—

SIR PETER

That you are a villain! And so I leave you to your conscience.

SURFACE

You are too rash, Sir Peter; you shall hear me. The man who   420
shuts out conviction by refusing to—

Exit SIR PETER *and* SURFACE, *talking*

Act V, Scene i

The Library in SURFACE's *house*
Enter [JOSEPH] SURFACE *and* SERVANT

SURFACE

Mr Stanley! And why should you think I would see him? You
must know he comes to ask something.

SERVANT

Sir, I should not have let him in, but that Mr Rowley came to
the door with him.

SURFACE

Pshaw! Blockhead! To suppose that I should now be in a   5
temper to receive visits from poor relations! Well, why don't
you show the fellow up?

SERVANT

I will, sir. Why sir, it was not my fault that Sir Peter discovered
my lady—

SURFACE

Go, fool!   10

[*Exit* SERVANT]

---

421 *conviction* Dublin 1780 inserts: SIR PETER Oh, damn your sentiments—damn your sen-
     timents!
     refusing to— Tickell, MSS (refusing to— SIR PETER Oh!   F Court, Georgetown in
     Sheridan's hand); a groan at Surface's speeches.
421 s.d. *Exit* SIR PETER *and* SURFACE, *talking* Tickell (*Exeunt*, SURFACE *following and speaking*
     F Court, Georgetown in Sheridan's hand; similar in other MSS)
  1 *And why* Tickell, MSS (Why   Georgetown). In this brisk opening to the scene, the
     audience grasps that Stanley's arrival has just been announced.

Sure, fortune never played a man of my policy such a trick
before. My character with Sir Peter, my hopes with Maria,
destroyed in a moment! I'm in a rare humour to listen to other
people's distresses. I shan't be able to bestow even a benevolent
sentiment on Stanley.—So here he comes and Rowley with   15
him. I must try to recover myself and put a little charity into
my face, however.   *Exit*

Enter SIR OLIVER [SURFACE] *and* ROWLEY

SIR OLIVER

What, does he avoid us? That was he, was it not?

ROWLEY

It was, sir. But I doubt you are come a little too abruptly. His
nerves are so weak that the sight of a poor relation may be too   20
much for him. I should have gone first to break it to him.

SIR OLIVER

Oh, plague of his nerves! Yet this is he whom Sir Peter extols as
a man of the most benevolent way of thinking.

ROWLEY

As to his way of thinking, I cannot pretend to decide; for, to do
him justice, he appears to have as much speculative   25
benevolence as any private gentleman in the kingdom, though
he is seldom so sensual as to indulge himself in the exercise of
it.

SIR OLIVER

Yet has a string of charitable sentiments at his fingers' ends.

ROWLEY

Or, rather, at his tongue's end, Sir Oliver, for I believe there is no   30
sentiment he has such faith in as that 'Charity begins at home'.

SIR OLIVER

And his, I presume, is of that domestic sort which never stirs
abroad at all.

ROWLEY

I doubt you'll find it so. But he's coming. I mustn't seem to

---

11 *policy* 'art; prudence; management of affairs', Johnson's *Dictionary*
17 *however* 'The use of "however" at the end of a sentence, though obsolete now,
    remained common in the late 18th and early 19th centuries.' (Bateson)
17 s.d. OLIVER Tickell, MSS (Oliver *as Old Stanley*   Crewe B)
21 *break it to him* Tickell (break you to him   MSS, Bateson)
25 *speculative* theoretical
29 *sentiments* Tickell, Spunge, Murray (sentiments I suppose   MSS, Bateson). Sir Oliver
    is not obliged to *suppose*; he extrapolates from what he has heard.

interrupt you; and you know immediately as you leave him, I   35
come in to announce your arrival in your real character.

SIR OLIVER

True, and afterwards you'll meet me at Sir Peter's.

ROWLEY

Without losing a moment.   *Exit*

SIR OLIVER

I don't like the complaisance of his features.

Enter [JOSEPH] SURFACE

SURFACE

Sir, I beg you ten thousand pardons for keeping you a moment   40
waiting. Mr Stanley, I presume.

SIR OLIVER

At your service.

SURFACE

Sir, I beg you will do me the honour to sit down.—I entreat
you, sir.

SIR OLIVER

Dear sir, there's no occasion. (*Aside*) Too civil by half.   45

SURFACE

I have not the pleasure of knowing you, Mr Stanley, but I am
extremely happy to see you look so well. You were nearly
related to my mother, I think, Mr Stanley?

SIR OLIVER

I was, sir; so nearly that my present poverty, I fear, may do
discredit to her wealthy children; else I should not have   50
presumed to trouble you.

SURFACE

Dear sir, there needs no apology. He that is in distress, though
a stranger, has a right to claim kindred with the wealthy. I am
sure I wish I was of that class and had it in my power to offer
you even a small relief.   55

SIR OLIVER

If your uncle, Sir Oliver, were here, I should have a friend.

SURFACE

I wish he was, sir, with all my heart. You should not want an
advocate with him, believe me, sir.

---

39   *complaisance* 'civility; desire of pleasing', Johnson's *Dictionary*

SIR OLIVER

I should not need one—my distresses would recommend me. But I imagined his bounty had enabled you to become the agent of his charity.   60

SURFACE

My dear sir, you were strangely misinformed. Sir Oliver is a worthy man, a very worthy man; but avarice, Mr Stanley, is the vice of age. I will tell you, my good sir, in confidence, what he has done for me has been a mere nothing; though people, I know, have thought otherwise, and for my part I never chose to contradict the report.   65

SIR OLIVER

What! Has he never transmitted you bullion—rupees, pagodas?

SURFACE

Oh, dear sir, nothing of the kind! No, no. A few presents now and then—china, shawls, congou tea, avadavats, and India crackers. Little more, believe me.   70

SIR OLIVER

[Aside] Here's gratitude for twelve thousand pounds! Avadavats and India crackers!

SURFACE

Then, my dear sir, you have heard, I doubt not, of the extravagance of my brother. There are very few would credit what I have done for that unfortunate young man.   75

SIR OLIVER

(Aside) Not I, for one.

SURFACE

The sums I have lent him! Indeed I have been exceedingly to blame. It was an amiable weakness; however, I don't pretend to defend it. And now I feel it doubly culpable, since it has deprived me of the pleasure of serving you, Mr Stanley, as my heart directs.   80

---

63 *a very worthy man* Tickell (a very worthy sort of man   MSS)
68 *pagodas* gold coins of Southern India
70 *congou tea* black China tea
    avadavats (avedevats   Tickell) Indian song-birds; 'Sheridan gave some to his first wife and wrote a mock elegy on the death of one of them' (Price, p. 425).
70–1 *India crackers* fireworks
77 s.d. *Aside* Georgetown, Crewe B, both in Sheridan's hand
79 *amiable* friendly, kindly
81 *pleasure* Tickell, Murray (power   MSS)

SIR OLIVER
[*Aside*] Dissembler! – Then, sir, you can't assist me?

SURFACE
At present, it grieves me to say, I cannot; but, whenever I have
the ability, you may depend upon hearing from me.   85

SIR OLIVER
I am extremely sorry—

SURFACE
Not more than I, believe me. To pity without the power to
relieve is still more painful than to ask and be denied.

SIR OLIVER
Kind sir, your most obedient humble servant.

SURFACE
You leave me deeply affected, Mr Stanley. William, be ready to   90
open the door.

SIR OLIVER
Oh, dear sir, no ceremony.

SURFACE
Your very obedient—

SIR OLIVER
Sir, your most obsequious—

SURFACE
You may depend upon hearing from me, whenever I can be of   95
service.

SIR OLIVER
Sweet sir, you are too good!

SURFACE
In the meantime, I wish you health and spirits.

SIR OLIVER
Your ever grateful and perpetual humble servant.

SURFACE
Sir, yours as sincerely.   100

SIR OLIVER
[*Aside*] Charles, you are my heir!   *Exit*

87–8   *To pity ... be denied* Joseph excels himself in his variation of 'This hurts me more than
it hurts you'.

90   Surface, claiming to be 'deeply affected' by Stanley's plight, for the first time addresses
his servant by name.

101   *Charles, you are my heir* Tickell, F Court, Lord C (Now I am satisfied   Georgetown,
Crewe B, Buck)

SURFACE

(*Solus*) This is one bad effect of a good character; it invites application from the unfortunate, and there needs no small degree of address to gain the reputation of benevolence without incurring the expense. The silver ore of pure charity is an   105
expensive article in the catalogue of a man's good qualities; whereas the sentimental French plate I use instead of it makes just as good a show and pays no tax.

Enter ROWLEY

ROWLEY

Mr Surface, your servant. I was apprehensive of interrupting you, though my business demands immediate attention—as   110
this note will inform you.

SURFACE

Always happy to see Mr Rowley. (*Reads the letter*) Sir Oliver Surface! My uncle arrived?

ROWLEY

He is, indeed. We have just parted. Quite well after a speedy voyage, and impatient to embrace his worthy nephew.   115

SURFACE

I am astonished. William, stop Mr Stanley, if he's not gone.

ROWLEY

Oh, he's out of reach, I believe.

SURFACE

Why did you not let me know this when you came in together?

ROWLEY

I thought you had particular business. But I must be gone to

---

102   s.d. *Solus* MSS except Lord C (not in Tickell, *Alone*   Bateson). Surface ends his soliloquy before Rowley enters and is not overheard, in contrast to IV.iii.18.

104   *address* skill

107   *sentimental French plate* In a neat analogy Surface boasts that his apparent benevolence costs him nothing. An annual tax on a household's silver had been introduced in 1756. 'French plate' (not in *OED*) refers presumably to inferior (possibly plated) silver-ware from France. For the suggestion that there is a play on sentimental comedy, also from France (*comédie larmoyante*) see Richard Brinsley Sheridan, *The School for Scandal and Other Plays*, ed. Michael Cordner (1998), p. 404.

112   *Mr Rowley* Tickell, MSS (Mr Rowley. (*Aside*) A rascal   Scott and other promptbooks). An actor's gag, Bateson suggests.

112–13   *Sir Oliver Surface!* Tickell (How! 'Oliver Surface!'   MSS)

inform your brother and appoint him here to meet your uncle.   120
He will be with you in a quarter of an hour.

SURFACE

So he says. Well, I am strangely overjoyed at his coming.
(*Aside*) Never to be sure was anything so damned unlucky!

ROWLEY

You will be delighted to see how well he looks.

SURFACE

Oh, I'm rejoiced to hear it. (*Aside*) Just at this time!   125

ROWLEY

I'll tell him how impatiently you expect him.   *Exit*

SURFACE

Do, do. Pray give my best duty and affection. Indeed, I cannot
express the sensations I feel at the thought of seeing him.
Certainly his coming just at this time is the cruellest piece of ill
fortune.   *Exit*   130

Act V, Scene ii

SIR PETER TEAZLE'S
Enter MRS CANDOUR *and* MAID

MAID

Indeed, ma'am, my lady will see nobody at present.

MRS CANDOUR

Did you tell her it was her friend Mrs Candour?

MAID

Yes, ma'am; but she begs you will excuse her.

MRS CANDOUR

Do go again. I shall be glad to see her if it be only for a
moment, for I am sure she must be in great distress.   5

[*Exit* MAID]

Dear heart, how provoking! I'm not mistress of half the
circumstances. We shall have the whole affair in the
newspapers, with the names of the parties at length, before I
have dropped the story at a dozen houses.

---

120   *to meet your* Tickell, Murray (to meet his   MSS)
125   s.d. *Aside* Georgetown, Buck
126   s.d. *Exit* Crewe B, Tickell (*Exit* ROWLEY   Buck). A long exit: as Rowley leaves Surface
can only express his feelings in double meanings.
  8   *at length* That is to say, not just initials, as in the Prologue, l. 14.

Enter SIR BENJAMIN BACKBITE

Oh, Sir Benjamin, you have heard, I suppose—   10

SIR BENJAMIN

Of Lady Teazle and Mr Surface—

MRS CANDOUR

And Sir Peter's discovery—

SIR BENJAMIN

Oh, the strangest piece of business, to be sure!

MRS CANDOUR

Well, I never was so surprised in my life. I am so sorry for all
parties, indeed.   15

SIR BENJAMIN

Now, I don't pity Sir Peter at all; he was so extravagantly partial
to Mr Surface.

MRS CANDOUR

Mr Surface! Why, 'twas with Charles Lady Teazle was detected.

SIR BENJAMIN

No, no, I tell you; Mr Surface is the gallant.

MRS CANDOUR

No such thing! Charles is the man. 'Twas Mr Surface brought   20
Sir Peter on purpose to discover them.

SIR BENJAMIN

I tell you I had it from one—

MRS CANDOUR

And I have it from one—

SIR BENJAMIN

Who had it from one, who had it—

MRS CANDOUR

From one immediately. But here comes Lady Sneerwell;   25
perhaps she knows the whole affair.

Enter LADY SNEERWELL

10 *Sir Benjamin* Tickell, Murray (dear Sir Benjamin   MSS)
15 *indeed* Tickell, MSS (indeed I am   Georgetown in Sheridan's hand, Bateson)
19 *No, no, I tell you* Tickell, Murray (No such thing   MSS)
20 *No such thing* Tickell, Murray (No, no   MSS)

LADY SNEERWELL

So, my dear Mrs Candour, here's a sad affair of our friend Teazle.

MRS CANDOUR

Aye, my dear friend, who would have thought—

LADY SNEERWELL

Well, there is no trusting appearances, though indeed she was   30
always too lively for me.

MRS CANDOUR

To be sure, her manners were a little too free; but then she was
so young!

LADY SNEERWELL

And had, indeed, some good qualities.

MRS CANDOUR

So she had, indeed. But have you heard the particulars?   35

LADY SNEERWELL

No; but everybody says that Mr Surface—

SIR BENJAMIN

Aye, there I told you Mr Surface was the man.

MRS CANDOUR

No, no; indeed, the assignation was with Charles.

LADY SNEERWELL

With Charles! You alarm me, Mrs Candour!

MRS CANDOUR

Yes, yes; he was the lover. Mr Surface, do him justice, was only   40
the informer.

SIR BENJAMIN

Well, I'll not dispute with you, Mrs Candour; but, be it which it
may, I hope that Sir Peter's wound will not—

MRS CANDOUR

Sir Peter's wound! Oh, mercy! I didn't hear a word of their fighting.

LADY SNEERWELL

Nor I, a syllable.   45

SIR BENJAMIN

No? What, no mention of the duel?

28 *Teazle* Tickell, Murray, MSS (Lady Teazle   Georgetown in Sheridan's hand). Inserting
'Lady' loses a realistic touch of female address but preserves a hypocritical politeness.
Geraldine Murray, 'A Sheridan Emendation', *N&Q*, Vol. 234 (New Series, Vol. 36)
No.4, Dec. 1989, 482–3, argues for 'our friend Teazle'.

33 *so young* Tickell (very young   MSS). Frances Abington was forty at the first performance, and Thomas King, Sir Peter, forty-seven.

MRS CANDOUR

Not a word.

SIR BENJAMIN

Oh Lord, yes. They fought before they left the room.

LADY SNEERWELL

Pray let us hear.

MRS CANDOUR

Aye, do oblige us with the duel.   50

SIR BENJAMIN

'Sir', says Sir Peter, immediately after the discovery, 'you are a
most ungrateful fellow'.

MRS CANDOUR

Aye, to Charles—

SIR BENJAMIN

No, no, to Mr Surface, 'a most ungrateful fellow; and, old as I
am, sir,' says he, 'I insist on immediate satisfaction.'   55

MRS CANDOUR

Aye, that must have been to Charles; for 'tis very unlikely Mr
Surface should go to fight in his own house.

SIR BENJAMIN

Gad's life, ma'am, not at all. 'Giving me immediate
satisfaction.' On this, ma'am, Lady Teazle, seeing Sir Peter in
such danger, ran out of the room in strong hysterics, and   60
Charles after her, calling out for hartshorn and water. Then,
madam, they began to fight with swords—

Enter CRABTREE

CRABTREE

With pistols, nephew—pistols. I have it from undoubted
authority.

MRS CANDOUR

Oh, Mr Crabtree, then it is all true?   65

CRABTREE

Too true, indeed, madam, and Sir Peter is dangerously
wounded.

---

48   *Oh Lord, yes* Tickell (O, Lord, yes, yes   MSS; Oh, yes   Murray)
61   *hartshorn* smelling salts, carbonate of ammonia
63   *pistols, nephew—pistols* Tickell, Murray (pistols, nephew   MSS)

SIR BENJAMIN

By a thrust in second quite through his left side—

CRABTREE

By a bullet lodged in the thorax.

MRS CANDOUR

Mercy on me! Poor Sir Peter!   70

CRABTREE

Yes, madam; though Charles would have avoided the matter, if he could.

MRS CANDOUR

I knew Charles was the person.

SIR BENJAMIN

My uncle, I see, knows nothing of the matter.

CRABTREE

But Sir Peter taxed him with the basest ingratitude.   75

SIR BENJAMIN

That I told you, you know—

CRABTREE

Do, nephew, let me speak—and insisted on an immediate—

SIR BENJAMIN

Just as I said—

CRABTREE

Odd's life, nephew, allow others to know something too. A pair of pistols lay on the bureau (for Mr Surface, it seems had come   80 there the night before late from Salthill, where he had been to see the Montem with a friend, who has a son at Eton) so, unluckily, the pistols were left charged.

SIR BENJAMIN

I heard nothing of this.

CRABTREE

Sir Peter forced Charles to take one, and they fired, it seems,   85

---

68 *second* Tickell (sécond(e)   MSS; segoon   Scott, Bateson) i.e. a thrust 'under the
    opponent's blade, and with the knuckles upward, the wrist turned downwards' (Price,
    p. 428). Though Sir Benjamin's technical term is comic in this context, swordsmanship
    was still a serious matter and a required accomplishment for a gentleman. Sheridan
    took lessons from a master fencer, and fought two duels.

81 *there the night before* Tickell (the night before   MSS)

82 *the Montem* the procession on Whit Tuesday every third year of Eton boys to Salt-Hill
    (the Montem, Latin for mountain), collecting money on the way for the school's
    Senior Scholar at King's College, Cambridge

83 *left charged* Because pistols took a long time to load travellers carried them ready
    loaded.

pretty nearly together. Charles's shot took place, as I told you, and Sir Peter's missed; but, what is very extraordinary, the ball struck against a little bronze Shakespeare that stood over the fireplace, grazed out of the window at a right angle, and wounded the postman, who was just coming to the door with a   90
double letter from Northamptonshire.

SIR BENJAMIN

My uncle's account is more circumstantial, I confess; but I believe mine is the true one, for all that.

LADY SNEERWELL

I am more interested in this affair than they imagine and must have better information.   *Exit*   95

SIR BENJAMIN

(*After a pause looking at each other*) Ah, Lady Sneerwell's alarm is very easily accounted for.

CRABTREE

Yes, yes, they certainly do say—but that's neither here nor there.

MRS CANDOUR

But, pray, where is Sir Peter at present?

CRABTREE

Oh, they brought him home, and he is now in the house,   100
though the servants are ordered to deny him.

MRS CANDOUR

I believe so, and Lady Teazle, I suppose, attending him.

CRABTREE

Yes, yes. I saw one of the faculty enter just before me.

SIR BENJAMIN

Hey! Who comes here?

CRABTREE

Oh, this is he—the physician, depend on't.   105

MRS CANDOUR

Oh, certainly. It must be the physician; and now we shall know.

Enter SIR OLIVER [SURFACE]

88   *little bronze Shakespeare* Tickell, Murray (little bronze Pliny   MSS, Bateson)
89   *fireplace* Tickell, Murray, F Court (chimney piece   MSS)
91   *double letter* 'written on two sheets and charged double postage' (Bateson)
96   s.d. *After a pause looking at each other* Georgetown, in Sheridan's hand
101 *deny him* Tickell (deny it MSS, Bateson)
103 *the faculty* the medical profession

CRABTREE
Well, doctor, what hopes?

MRS CANDOUR
Aye, doctor, how's your patient?

SIR BENJAMIN
Now, doctor, isn't it a wound with a small sword?

CRABTREE
A bullet lodged in the thorax, for a hundred!   110

SIR OLIVER
Doctor! A wound with a small sword! And a bullet in the thorax? Oons! Are you mad, good people?

SIR BENJAMIN
Perhaps, sir, you are not a doctor?

SIR OLIVER
Truly, I am to thank you for my degree, if I am.

CRABTREE
Only a friend of Sir Peter's, then, I presume. But, sir, you must   115
have heard of his accident.

SIR OLIVER
Not a word!

CRABTREE
Not of his being dangerously wounded?

SIR OLIVER
The devil he is!

SIR BENJAMIN
Run through the body—   120

CRABTREE
Shot in the breast—

SIR BENJAMIN
By one Mr Surface—

CRABTREE
Aye, the younger.

SIR OLIVER
Hey! What the plague! You seem to differ strangely in your accounts. However you agree that Sir Peter is dangerously   125
wounded.

SIR BENJAMIN
Oh, yes, we agree there.

110   *for a hundred* i.e. betting £100 that he has the facts
116   *his accident* Tickell, Georgetown (this accident   MSS)

CRABTREE

Yes, yes, I believe there can be no doubt of that.

SIR OLIVER

Then, upon my word, for a person in that situation he is the most imprudent man alive; for here he comes, walking as if   130
nothing at all was the matter.

Enter SIR PETER TEAZLE

Odd's heart, Sir Peter, you are come in good time, I promise you; for we had just given you over.

SIR BENJAMIN

Egad, uncle, this is the most sudden recovery!

SIR OLIVER

Why, man, what do you do out of bed with a small sword   135
through your body, and a bullet lodged in your thorax?

SIR PETER

A small sword, and a bullet!

SIR OLIVER

Aye, these gentlemen would have killed you without law or physic, and wanted to dub me a doctor to make me an accomplice.   140

SIR PETER

Why, what is all this?

SIR BENJAMIN

We rejoice, Sir Peter, that the story of the duel is not true and are sincerely sorry for your other misfortune.

SIR PETER

(*Aside*) So, so. All over the town already.

CRABTREE

Though, Sir Peter, you were certainly vastly to blame to marry   145
at all at your years.

SIR PETER

Sir, what business is that of yours?

MRS CANDOUR

Though, indeed, as Sir Peter made so good a husband, he's very much to be pitied

131   *was* Tickell, Lord C, Crewe B, Buck (were   Georgetown in Sheridan's hand)
138–9   *without law or physic* traditional satirical jibe at lawyers and doctors profiting by death and illness
144   s.d. *Aside* Georgetown in Sheridan's hand

SIR PETER

Plague on your pity, ma'am! I desire none of it.   150

SIR BENJAMIN

However, Sir Peter, you must not mind the laughing and jests
you will meet with on the occasion.

SIR PETER

Sir, sir, I desire to be master in my own house.

CRABTREE

'Tis no uncommon case; that's one comfort.

SIR PETER

I insist on being left to myself. Without ceremony, I insist on   155
your leaving my house directly!

MRS CANDOUR

Well, well, we are going—and depend on't, we'll make the best
report of it we can.

SIR PETER

Leave my house!

CRABTREE

And tell how hardly you have been treated.   160

SIR PETER

Leave my house!

SIR BENJAMIN

And how patiently you bear it.

SIR PETER

Fiends! Vipers! Furies! Oh, that their own venom would choke
them!

Exeunt MRS CANDOUR, SIR BENJAMIN [BACKBITE], CRABTREE

SIR OLIVER

They are very provoking indeed, Sir Peter.   165

Enter ROWLEY

ROWLEY

I heard high words—what has ruffled you, Sir Peter?

SIR PETER

Pshaw! What signifies asking? Do I ever pass a day without my
vexations?

152 *the occasion* Tickell, Lord C, Buck (this occasion   Georgetown, Crewe B)
154 *one comfort* MSS (my comfort   Tickell). A copyist's error.
158 *of it* Tickell (of you   MSS). Perhaps another copyist error.
166 *high* loud

SIR OLIVER

Well, I'm not inquisitive. I come only to tell you that I have
seen both my nephews, in the manner we proposed.   170

SIR PETER

A precious couple they are!

ROWLEY

Yes, and Sir Oliver is convinced that your judgment was right,
Sir Peter.

SIR OLIVER

Yes, I find Joseph is indeed the man, after all.

ROWLEY

Aye, as Sir Peter says, he is a Man of Sentiment.   175

SIR OLIVER

And acts up to the sentiments he professes.

ROWLEY

It certainly is edification to hear him talk.

SIR OLIVER

O, he's a model for the young men of the age! But how's this,
Sir Peter, you don't join in your friend Joseph's praise, as I
expected?   180

SIR PETER

Sir Oliver, we live in a damned wicked world, and the fewer we
praise the better.

ROWLEY

What, do you say so, Sir Peter, who were never mistaken in
your life?

SIR PETER

Pshaw! Plague on you both! I see by your sneering you have   185
heard the whole affair. I shall go mad among you.

ROWLEY

Then, to fret you no longer, Sir Peter, we are indeed acquainted
with it all. I met Lady Teazle coming from Mr Surface's so
humbled that she deigned to request me to be her advocate
with you.   190

SIR PETER

And does Sir Oliver know all this?

SIR OLIVER

Every circumstance.

175–8 Quoting his own words back to him from I.ii.51–3, II.iii.59–60.

SIR PETER
　What? Of the closet and the screen, hey?
SIR OLIVER
　Yes, yes, and the little French milliner. Oh, I have been vastly
　diverted with the story! Ha, ha, ha, ha!   195
SIR PETER
　'Twas very pleasant.
SIR OLIVER
　I never laughed more in my life, I assure you. Ha, ha, ha!
SIR PETER
　Oh, vastly diverting. Ha, ha, ha!
ROWLEY
　To be sure, Joseph with his sentiments! Ha, ha!
SIR PETER
　Yes, yes, his sentiments! Ha, ha, ha! Hypocritical villain.   200
SIR OLIVER
　Aye, and that rogue Charles to pull Sir Peter out of the closet!
　Ha, ha, ha!
SIR PETER
　Ha, ha! 'Twas devilish entertaining, to be sure.
SIR OLIVER
　Ha, ha, ha! Egad, Sir Peter, I should like to have seen your face
　when the screen was thrown down. Ha, ha!   205
SIR PETER
　Yes, yes, my face when the screen was thrown down. Ha, ha,
　ha! Oh, I must never show my head again.
SIR OLIVER
　But, come, come, it isn't fair to laugh at you neither, my old
　friend, though, upon my soul, I can't help it.
SIR PETER
　Oh, pray don't restrain your mirth on my account. It does not   210
　hurt me at all. I laugh at the whole affair myself. Yes, yes, I
　think being a standing jest for all one's acquaintance a very
　happy situation. Oh, yes, and then of a morning to read the

196　*pleasant* amusing
199　*Ha, ha!* Only enough space on the line this time for two Ha-s.

paragraphs about Mr S——, Lady T——, and Sir P—— will be so
entertaining.   215

ROWLEY

Without affectation, Sir Peter, you may despise the ridicule of
fools. But I see Lady Teazle going towards the next room. I am
sure you must desire a reconciliation as earnestly as she does.

SIR OLIVER

Perhaps my being here prevents her coming to you. Well, I'll
leave honest Rowley to mediate between you; but he must   220
bring you all presently to Mr Surface's, where I am now
returning, if not to reclaim a libertine, at least to expose
hypocrisy.   *Exit*

SIR PETER

Ah, I'll be present at your discovering yourself there with all my
heart, though 'tis a vile unlucky place for discoveries.   225

ROWLEY

We'll follow.

SIR PETER

She is not coming here, you see, Rowley.

ROWLEY

No, but she has left the door of that room open, you perceive.
See, she is in tears.

SIR PETER

Certainly a little mortification appears very becoming in a wife.   230
Don't you think it will do her good to let her pine a little?

ROWLEY

Oh, this is ungenerous in you.

---

215   *entertaining* Georgetown, Buck, Tickell, Murray (entertaining. I shall certainly leave
        town tomorrow and never look mankind in the face again!   F Court, Lord C, Crewe
        B, Scott). Scott and other promptbooks reveal that this comically exaggerated misan-
        thropy survived on stage, as did Lady Sneerwell's threatened appearance in IV.iii; see
        note at IV.iii.324.

223   s.d. *Exit* Tickell, Crewe B (*Exit* SIR OLIVER Buck); another long exit.

224   *discovering* revealing

225   *discoveries* Tickell, MSS (discoveries. SIR OLIVER However, it is very convenient to the
        carrying on of my plot that you all live so near one another! *Exit*   F Court, Lord C).
        This is a sudden and distracting concern with the plausibility of the action.

229   *tears* Tickell, MSS (tears. SIR PETER She seems indeed to wish that I should go to her—
        how dejected she appears. ROWLEY And will you refrain from comforting her?   F
        Court, Lord C)

SIR PETER

Well, I know not what to think. You remember, Rowley, the letter I found of hers evidently intended for Charles?

ROWLEY

A mere forgery, Sir Peter, laid in your way on purpose. This is   235
one of the points which I intend Snake shall give you conviction of.

SIR PETER

I wish I were once satisfied of that. She looks this way. What a remarkably elegant turn of the head she has! Rowley, I'll go to her.   240

ROWLEY

Certainly.

SIR PETER

Though, when it is known that we are reconciled, people will laugh at me ten times more.

ROWLEY

Let them laugh, and retort their malice only by showing them you are happy in spite of it.   245

SIR PETER

I'faith, so I will! And, if I'm not mistaken, we may yet be the happiest couple in the country.

ROWLEY

Nay, Sir Peter, he who once lays aside suspicion—

SIR PETER

Hold, Master Rowley! If you have any regard for me, never let me hear you utter anything like a sentiment. I have had enough   250
of them to serve me the rest of my life.

Exeunt

Act V, Scene the last [iii]

The Library in SURFACE*'s house*
Enter [JOSEPH] SURFACE *and* LADY SNEERWELL

LADY SNEERWELL

Impossible! Will not Sir Peter immediately be reconciled to

---

249   *Hold, Master Rowley!* Tickell, MSS (Hold, my dear Rowley   Crewe B in Sheridan's hand). This is a delicate suggestion of Sir Peter's softening mood.

Charles and, of course, no longer oppose his union with Maria? The thought is distraction to me.

SURFACE

Can passion furnish a remedy?

LADY SNEERWELL

No, nor cunning neither. Oh, I was a fool, an idiot, to league   5
with such a blunderer!

SURFACE

Sure, Lady Sneerwell, I am the greatest sufferer; yet you see I bear the accident with calmness.

LADY SNEERWELL

Because the disappointment doesn't reach your heart; your interest only attached you to Maria. Had you felt for her what I   10
have for that ungrateful libertine, neither your temper nor hypocrisy could prevent your showing the sharpness of your vexation.

SURFACE

But why should your reproaches fall on me for this disappointment?   15

LADY SNEERWELL

Are you not the cause of it? What had you to do to bate in your pursuit of Maria, to pervert Lady Teazle by the way? Had you not a sufficient field for your roguery in blinding Sir Peter, and supplanting your brother? I hate such an avarice of crimes; 'tis an unfair monopoly, and never prospers.   20

SURFACE

Well, I admit I have been to blame. I confess I deviated from the direct road of wrong, but I don't think we're so totally defeated neither.

LADY SNEERWELL

No!

---

2 *of course* Tickell, Murray (of consequence   MSS). Bateson comments: 'an idiom of melodrama rather than polite conversation'.

4 *Can passion furnish a remedy?* i. e. Can being in a rage help you? Compare Surface's own 'calmness' l. 8.

5 *neither* Tickell (either   MSS)

16 *Are you not* Tickell (Are not you   MSS)

16-7 *What ... the way?* Tickell, MSS (not in Murray)
    bate slacken

18 *blinding* Tickell, MSS (imposing upon   Murray, Bateson)

19 *brother* Tickell, MSS (brother, but you must endeavour to seduce his wife   Murray, Bateson)

SURFACE

You tell me you have made a trial of Snake since we met, and   25
that you still believe him faithful to us?

LADY SNEERWELL

I do believe so.

SURFACE

And that he has undertaken, should it be necessary, to swear
and prove that Charles is at this time contracted by vows and
honour to your ladyship—which some of his former letters to   30
you will serve to support.

LADY SNEERWELL

This, indeed, might have assisted.

SURFACE

Come, come; it is not too late yet. (*Knocking at the door*) But
hark! This is probably my uncle, Sir Oliver. Retire to that room;
we'll consult farther when he is gone.   35

LADY SNEERWELL

Well, but if *he* should find you out too?

SURFACE

Oh, I have no fear of that. Sir Peter will hold his tongue for his
own credit's sake—and you may depend on it I shall soon
discover Sir Oliver's weak side!

LADY SNEERWELL

I have no diffidence of your abilities. Only be constant to one   40
roguery at a time.   *Exit*

SURFACE

I will, I will! So! 'tis confounded hard, after such bad fortune,
to be baited by one's confederate in evil. Well, at all events my
character is so much better than Charles's that I certainly—hey!
What? This is not Sir Oliver but old Stanley again. Plague on't   45
that he should return to tease me just now. We shall have Sir
Oliver come and find him here and—

Enter SIR OLIVER [SURFACE]

Gad's life, Mr Stanley, why have you come back to plague me at
this time? You must not stay now, upon my word.

---

33   s.d. *Knocking at the door* Crewe B, Buck
40   *diffidence of* lack of confidence in
43   *baited* harassed, tormented

SIR OLIVER

> Sir, I hear your uncle Oliver is expected here, and though he   50
> has been so penurious to you, I'll try what he'll do for me.

SURFACE

> Sir, 'tis impossible for you to stay now, so I must beg—come
> any other time, and I promise you, you shall be assisted.

SIR OLIVER

> No. Sir Oliver and I must be acquainted.

SURFACE

> Zounds, sir! Then I insist on your quitting the room directly.   55

SIR OLIVER

> Nay, sir—

SURFACE

> Sir, I insist on't. Here, William! Show this gentleman out. Since
> you compel me, sir, not one moment. This is such insolence.
>
> *Going to push him out*

Enter CHARLES [SURFACE]

CHARLES

> Hey day! What is the matter now? What the devil, have you got
> hold of my little broker here? Zounds, brother, don't hurt little   60
> Premium. What's the matter, my little fellow?

SURFACE

> So! he has been with you too, has he?

CHARLES

> To be sure he has. Why, he's as honest a little—but sure,
> Joseph, you have not been borrowing money too, have you?

SURFACE

> Borrowing? No, but, brother, you know here we—expect Sir   65
> Oliver every—

CHARLES

> O Gad, that's true! Noll mustn't find the little broker here, to
> be sure.

SURFACE

> Yet, Mr Stanley insists—

CHARLES

> Stanley! Why, his name's Premium.   70

65–6   *here we—expect Sir Oliver every* Tickell, MSS (we expect Sir Oliver here   Murray).
Perhaps Surface's agitation produces the pauses and awkward word order.

SURFACE
  No, sir, Stanley.
CHARLES
  No, no, Premium.
SURFACE
  Well, no matter which. But—
CHARLES
  Aye, aye, Stanley or Premium, 'tis the same thing, as you say;
  for I suppose he goes by half a hundred names, besides A. B. at   75
  the coffee-house.   *Knocking*
SURFACE
  'Sdeath! here's Sir Oliver at the door. (*Knocking again*) Now I
  beg, Mr Stanley—
CHARLES
  Aye, aye, and I beg, Mr Premium—
SIR OLIVER
  Gentlemen—   80
SURFACE
  Sir, by Heaven, you shall go.
CHARLES
  Aye, out with him, certainly.
SIR OLIVER
  This violence—
SURFACE
  Sir, 'tis your own fault.
CHARLES
  Out with him, to be sure.   85

                              Both forcing SIR OLIVER *out*

              Enter SIR PETER *and* LADY TEAZLE, MARIA, *and* ROWLEY
SIR PETER
  My old friend, Sir Oliver—hey! What in the name of wonder?
  Here are dutiful nephews—assault their uncle at a first visit.
LADY TEAZLE
  Indeed, Sir Oliver, 'twas well we came in to rescue you.

75–6 *A. B. at the coffee-house* initials to which messages could be addressed
76 s.d. *Knocking* Tickell, Crewe B (*Knock* F Court; other MSS have *Knock(ing)* after
      'door' (l. 77), *Knocking again* Crewe B, in Sheridan's hand)

ROWLEY

Truly it was; for I perceive, Sir Oliver, the character of old Stanley was no protection to you.   90

SIR OLIVER

Nor of Premium either. The necessities of the former could not extort a shilling from that benevolent gentleman: and now, egad, I stood a chance of faring worse than my ancestors and being knocked down without being bid for.

After a pause, SURFACE *and* CHARLES *turning to each other*

SURFACE

Charles!   95

CHARLES

Joseph!

SURFACE

'Tis now complete.

CHARLES

Very!

SIR OLIVER

Sir Peter, my friend, and Rowley too, look on that elder nephew of mine. You know what he has already received from   100 my bounty; and you know also how gladly I would have regarded half my fortune as held in trust for him. Judge then my disappointment in discovering him to be destitute of faith, charity, and gratitude.

SIR PETER

Sir Oliver, I should be more surprised at this declaration if I   105 had not myself found him to be mean, treacherous, and hypocritical.

LADY TEAZLE

And if the gentleman pleads not guilty to these, pray let him call *me* to his character.

SIR PETER

Then, I believe, we need add no more. If he knows himself, he   110

---

94 s.d. *After a pause,* SURFACE *and* CHARLES *turning to each other* Crewe B, in Sheridan's hand

103 *faith* Tickell, Murray (truth   MSS, Bateson). Possibly a copyist's slip; *faith* here would mean being faithful, keeping one's word.

106 *mean* Tickell, Murray (selfish   MSS)

109 *call* me *to* i.e. ask *me* to speak about

[162]

will consider it as the most perfect punishment that he is
known by the world.

CHARLES

(*Aside*) If they talk this way to honesty, what will they say to *me*
by and by?

SIR OLIVER

As for that prodigal, his brother there—   115

CHARLES

(*Aside*) Aye, now comes my turn. The damned family pictures
will ruin me.

SURFACE

Sir Oliver, Uncle, will you honour me with a hearing?

CHARLES

(*Aside*) Now, if Joseph would make one of his long speeches,
and I might recollect myself a little.   120

SIR OLIVER

I suppose you would undertake to justify yourself entirely?

SURFACE

I trust I could.

SIR OLIVER

Well, sir, and you (*To* CHARLES) could justify yourself *too*, I
suppose?

CHARLES

Not that I know of, Sir Oliver.   125

SIR OLIVER

What? Little Premium has been let too much into the secret, I
suppose?

CHARLES

True, sir; but they were *family secrets* and should not be
mentioned again, you know.

ROWLEY

Come, Sir Oliver, I know you cannot speak of Charles's follies   130
with anger.

113, 116, 119 s.d. *Aside* Georgetown in Sheridan's hand

120   *and I* Tickell, F Court, Lord C (I   Georgetown, Crewe B, Buck)

123   *Well, sir* Tickell, Murray (Pshaw! Well, sir   Georgetown; Pshaw! Nay if you desert
your roguery in its distress, and try to be justified, you have even less principle than I
thought you had   other MSS). Sir Peter's rebuke is retained in some promptbooks.

123   s.d. *To* CHARLES Georgetown, in Sheridan's hand

128   *not be* Tickell, Murray (never be   MSS)

SIR OLIVER

Odd's heart, no more I can—nor with gravity either. Sir Peter, do you know the rogue bargained with me for all his ancestors, sold me judges and generals by the foot and maiden aunts as cheap as broken china?   135

CHARLES

To be sure, Sir Oliver, I did make a little free with the family canvas, that's the truth on't. My ancestors may certainly rise in judgment against me, there's no denying it. But believe me sincere when I tell you, and upon my soul I would not say it if I was not, that if I do not appear mortified at the exposure of my   140 follies, it is because I feel at this moment the warmest satisfaction in seeing you, my liberal benefactor.

SIR OLIVER

Charles, I believe you. Give me your hand again. The ill-looking little fellow over the settee has made your peace.

CHARLES

Then, sir, my gratitude to the original is still increased.   145

LADY TEAZLE

Yet I believe, Sir Oliver, here is one whom Charles is still more anxious to be reconciled to.

SIR OLIVER

Oh, I have heard of his attachment there; and, with the young lady's pardon, if I construe right, that blush—

SIR PETER

Well, child, speak your sentiments!   150

MARIA

Sir, I have little to say, but that I shall rejoice to hear that he is happy. For me, whatever claim I had to his affection, I willingly resign to one who has a better title.

CHARLES

How, Maria!

134–5 *sold me judges ... broken china?* In F Court the lines follow 'old tapestry' (IV.ii.9). Here Sheridan notes: 'N.B. to be altered in the 4th Act'. (In Lord C the passage appears in both places.) Dividing Sir Oliver's comic comparisons makes them more effective: they are witty enough to work singly or in a group of two, and the lines here recall the earlier occasion.

138 *judgment* Tickell, Murray (evidence   MSS)

144 *settee* Tickell, MSS (couch   F Court, Lord C)
      peace Tickell (peace, sirrah!   Crewe B in Sheridan's hand)

153 *resign* Tickell, Murray, MSS (resign it   Georgetown in Sheridan's hand)

SIR PETER

> Hey day! What's the mystery now? When he appeared an   155
> incorrigible rake, you would give your hand to no one else; and
> now that he is likely to reform, I'll warrant you won't have him.

MARIA

> His own heart and Lady Sneerwell know the cause.

CHARLES

> Lady Sneerwell!

SURFACE

> Brother, it is with great concern I am obliged to speak on this   160
> point, but my regard to justice obliges me, and Lady
> Sneerwell's injuries can no longer be concealed. *Opens the door*

Enter LADY SNEERWELL

SIR PETER

> So another French milliner! Egad, he has one in every room in
> the house, I suppose.

LADY SNEERWELL

> Ungrateful Charles! Well may you be surprised, and feel for the   165
> indelicate situation which your perfidy has forced me into.

CHARLES

> Pray, Uncle, is this another plot of yours? For, as I have life, I
> don't understand it.

SURFACE

> I believe, sir, there is but the evidence of one person more
> necessary to make it extremely clear.   170

SIR PETER

> And that person, I imagine, is Mr Snake. Rowley, you were
> perfectly right to bring him with us, and pray let him appear.

ROWLEY

> Walk in, Mr Snake.

Enter SNAKE

> I thought his testimony might be wanted; however, it happens
> unluckily, that he comes to confront Lady Sneerwell, not to   175
> support her.

---

161 *obliges* Tickell, MSS (compels   Georgetown in Sheridan's hand, Bateson)
173 s.d. *Enter* SNAKE Moving Snake's revelations from III.i to here means they are now
made in Lady Sneerwell's presence, and link the end of the play with the opening scene.

LADY SNEERWELL

A villain! (*Aside*) Treacherous to me at last! – Speak, fellow, have you too conspired against me?

SNAKE

I beg your ladyship ten thousand pardons. You paid me extremely liberally for the lie in question; but I have   180 unfortunately been offered double to speak the truth.

SIR PETER

Plot and counterplot, egad!

LADY SNEERWELL

The torments of shame and disappointment on you all!

LADY TEAZLE

Hold, Lady Sneerwell. Before you go, let me thank you for the trouble you and that gentleman have taken in writing letters   185 from me to Charles, and answering them yourself. And let me also request you make my respects to the scandalous college of which you are president, and inform them, that Lady Teazle, licentiate, begs leave to return the diploma they gave her, as she leaves off practice and kills characters no longer.   190

LADY SNEERWELL

You too, madam! Provoking insolent! May your husband live these fifty years.   *Exit*

SIR PETER

Oons! what a Fury!

LADY TEAZLE

A malicious creature indeed!

SIR PETER

Hey! Not for her last wish?   195

LADY TEAZLE

Oh, no!

SIR OLIVER

Well, sir, and what have you to say now?

177 *A villian* Tickell, MSS (Villain   Georgetown in Sheridan's hand)
177 s.d. *Aside* Georgetown, in Sheridan's hand
182 *egad* Tickell, MSS (egad. I wish your ladyship joy of the success of your negotiation Georgetown)
186 *from me to Charles* Tickell, Murray (to me from Charles   MSS). See the earlier reference to forged letters implicating Lady Teazle, whether by or to her, at III.i.39–41.
189 *gave* Tickell (granted   MSS)
194 *A malicious ... indeed* Tickell, MSS (What a malicious creature it is! Crewe B in Sheridan's hand, Bateson)

SURFACE

Sir, I am so confounded to find that Lady Sneerwell could be guilty of suborning Mr Snake in this manner to impose on us all, that I know not what to say. However, lest her revengeful   200
spirit should prompt her to injure my brother I had certainly better follow her directly.   *Exit*

SIR PETER

Moral to the last drop!

SIR OLIVER

Aye, and marry her, Joseph, if you can. Oil and vinegar, egad! You'll do very well together.   205

ROWLEY

I believe we have no more occasion for Mr Snake at present.

SNAKE

Before I go, I beg pardon once for all for whatever uneasiness I have been the humble instrument of causing to the parties present.

SIR PETER

Well, well, you have made atonement by a good deed at last.   210

SNAKE

But I must request of the company that it shall never be known.

SIR PETER

Hey! What the plague! Are you ashamed of having done a right thing once in your life?

SNAKE

Ah, sir, consider. I live by the badness of my character. I have   215
nothing but my infamy to depend on, and, if it were once known that I had been betrayed into an honest action, I should lose every friend I have in the world.

SIR OLIVER

Well, well, we'll not traduce you by saying anything in your praise, never fear.   220

Exit SNAKE

SIR PETER

There's a precious rogue!

---

221 *rogue* Tickell (rogue—yet that fellow is a writer and a critic. F Court, Lord C, Georgetown, Bateson). For possible identifications of Snake, see p. 18.

LADY TEAZLE

See, Sir Oliver. There needs no persuasion now to reconcile your nephew and Maria.

CHARLES *and* MARIA *apart*

SIR OLIVER

Aye, aye, that's as it should be, and, egad, we'll have the wedding tomorrow morning.   225

CHARLES

Thank you, dear Uncle.

SIR PETER

What, you rogue, don't you ask the girl's consent first?

CHARLES

Oh, I have done that a long time—a minute ago—and she has looked yes.

MARIA

For shame, Charles! I protest, Sir Peter, there has not been a   230
word.

SIR OLIVER

Well then, the fewer the better. May your love for each other never know abatement!

. SIR PETER

And may you live as happily together as Lady Teazle and I— intend to do!   235

CHARLES

Rowley, my old friend, I am sure you congratulate me; and I suspect that I owe you much.

SIR OLIVER

You do, indeed, Charles.

ROWLEY

If my efforts to serve you had not succeeded, you would have been in my debt for the attempt; but deserve to be happy and   240
you overpay me.

SIR PETER

Aye, honest Rowley always said you would reform.

---

223 s.d. CHARLES *and* MARIA *apart* Lord C, Georgetown, i. e. standing together at a distance from the others
228 *a minute ago* Tickell (above *or* about a minute ago   MSS)

[168]

CHARLES

> Why, as to reforming, Sir Peter, I'll make no promises, and that
> I take to be a proof that I intend to set about it. But here shall
> be my monitor, my gentle guide. Ah, can I leave the virtuous   245
> path those eyes illumine?

> > Though thou, dear maid, should'st waive thy beauty's sway,
> > Thou still must rule, because I will obey;
> > An humbled fugitive from folly view,
> > No sanctuary near—but love, and you.   250

> > > *(To the audience)*

> > You can, indeed, each anxious fear remove,
> > For even scandal dies, if you approve!

243–4 *Why, as to reforming . . . about it* In a letter to his father of 1772 Sheridan spoke of aban-
   doning his 'habit of dissipation' in remarkably similar words: 'I believe the best speci-
   men I can give you of a prospect of my reforming wholly in this point, is to avoid
   professing anything on the subject.' (*Letters*, I, 35)
250 s.d. *To the audience* Tickell, Georgetown; placed after *approve* (l. 252) in Crewe B, Buck.
   Sheridan made a joke of the pressure and anxiety surrounding the completing of the
   play in his last words in the F Court MS: 'Finished. Thank God! R. B. S.—Amen! W.
   Hopkins'. Hopkins was Prompter at Drury Lane, and responsible, among many tasks,
   for making up the promptbook, and copying out the actors' parts.

EPILOGUE

[*Written*] *by Mr Colman*

[*Spoken by*] LADY TEAZLE

I, who was late so volatile and gay,
Like a trade-wind must now blow all one way,
Bend all my cares, my studies, and my vows,
To one old rusty weathercock—my spouse!
So wills our virtuous bard—the motley Bayes   5
Of crying epilogues and laughing plays.
Old bachelors who marry smart young wives
Learn from our play to regulate your lives.
Each bring his dear to town, all faults upon her—
London will prove the very source of honour.   10
Plunged fairly in, like a cold bath it serves,
When principles relax, to brace the nerves.
Such is my case; and yet I might deplore
That the gay dream of dissipation's o'er.
And say, ye fair, was ever lively wife,   15
Born with a genius for the highest life,

---

by ... Mr Colman Tickell (Written by G. Coleman, Esqr. Georgetown in
Sheridan's hand; written by Mr. Coleman Buck in Sheridan's hand). George
Colman the Elder (1732–94) was, like Sheridan, both dramatist and London theatre
manager.

LADY TEAZLE Tickell (Spoken by Mrs. Abington Lord C, Georgetown; in the Character
of Lady Teazle Lord C). The Epilogue was usually entrusted to one of the principal
characters who would then comment on or even, as here, question the role they had
played. 'Mrs Abington had been a favourite epilogist of Garrick's.' (Bateson)

4 *old* Tickell, MSS (dull Murray)

5 *virtuous bard* Sheridan is *virtuous* in writing a play which upholds marriage: husband
and wife are reconciled, Lady Teazle condemns Surface's attempt at seduction and
gives up scandalmongering. But her questioning of his prescription of wifely virtue
runs through the Epilogue.

motley Bayes The phrase identifies Sheridan as a writer of comedies. *Motley* is the
multi-coloured suit of the Fool, and therefore connotes comedy. Bayes is the playwright in Buckingham's brilliant burlesque, *The Rehearsal*, a satirical figure of John
Dryden, first poet laureate and writer of heroic dramas, with *Bayes* alluding to the
wreath of bay or laurel leaves awarded to a Classical poet. *The Rehearsal* was 'clearly
Sheridan's major inspiration' when he wrote *The Critic.*' Crane, p. xiii.

6 *crying epilogues* Referring to Sheridan's recent sentimental epilogue to George
Ayscough's *Semiramis* (Drury Lane, December 1776).

Like me untimely blasted in her bloom,
Like me condemned to such a dismal doom?
Save money, when I just knew how to waste it!
Leave London, just as I began to taste it!   20
Must I then watch the early crowing cock,
The melancholy ticking of a clock
In a lone rustic hall forever pounded,
With dogs, cats, rats, and squalling brats surrounded?
With humble curates can I now retire   25
(While good Sir Peter boozes with the squire)
And at backgammon mortify my soul,
That pants for loo or flutters at a vole?
'Seven's the main!'—dear sound that must expire,
Lost at hot cockles round a Christmas fire.   30
The transient hour of fashion too soon spent,

20 *Leave London* In the play it is not clear that this is to be her fate, but the idea allows
    Colman to conjure up yet another composite image of dull rural life, ll. 21–30.
28 *loo* round game where players are dealt three or five cards
    vole winning all the tricks in ombre, quadrille, etc.
29 *'Seven's the main!'* in hazard, i.e. dice, the 'main' is the winning number nominated by
    the caster.
30 *hot cockles* a country, or Christmas, game where one player is blindfolded and then
    kneels down and has to guess who strikes him on the back; mentioned in Goldsmith's
    The Vicar of Wakefield, ch. xi.

Farewell the tranquil mind, farewell content!
Farewell the plumèd head, the cushioned tête,
That takes the cushion from its proper seat!
The spirit-stirring drum, (card drums, I mean—   35
Spadille, odd trick, pam, basto, king and queen!)
And you, ye knockers that with brazen throat
The welcome visitors' approach denote.
Farewell all quality of high renown,
Pride, pomp and circumstance of glorious town!   40
Farewell! Your revels I partake no more,
And Lady Teazle's occupation's o'er!
All this I told our bard; he smiled and said 'twas clear
I ought to play deep tragedy next year.
Meanwhile he drew wise morals from his play   45
And in these solemn periods stalked away:
'Blessed were the fair like you, her faults who stopped,
And closed her follies when the curtain dropped—
No more in vice or error to engage
Or play the fool at large on life's great stage'.   50

32–42 Parodying Othello's farewell to his military profession, *Othello*, III.iii.349–58.
    33 *cushioned tête* head of hair, or wig, built up high on pads
    35 *card drums* private evening card parties
    36 *Spadille* ace of spades in ombre
        pam knave of clubs in loo, the highest trump
        basto ace of clubs in quadrille or ombre
    43 *our bard* Sheridan is imagined responding to Mrs Abington's lament by suggesting she
        is ready to play *deep tragedy next year*. In fact, she played only comic roles, and was
        painted by Reynolds as 'the muse of comedy'.
47–50 '*Blessed . . . stage*' For a 'certain piquancy' in the recommendation that women imitate
        Lady Teazle being spoken by Mrs Abington see p. 30.

NOTES

NOTES

NOTES

NOTES

NOTES

NOTES

NOTES

NOTES

NOTES

NOTES

NOTES